Fashion
Buying

Helen Goworek
Senior Lecturer, Nottingham Trent University

Blackwell
Science

© 2001 by Blackwell Science Ltd, a Blackwell Publishing company
Editorial offices:
Blackwell Science Ltd, 9600 Garsington Road, Oxford OX4 2DQ, UK
    Tel: +44 (0) 1865 776868
Blackwell Publishing Inc., 350 Main Street, Malden, MA 02148-5020, USA
    Tel: +1 781 388 8250
Blackwell Science Asia Pty Ltd, 550 Swanston Street, Carlton, Victoria 3053, Australia
    Tel: +61 (0)3 8359 1011

First published 2001
Reprinted 2004

Library of Congress Cataloging-in-Publication Data
Goworek, Helen.
    Fashion buying / Helen Goworek.
        p. cm.
    Includes bibliographical references and
index
    ISBN 0-632-05584-7
        1. Fashion merchandising. 2. Vocational
guidance. 3. Purchasing. 4. Clothing
trade. I. Title.

HD9940.A2 G68 2001
391'.0068'7—dc21   2001043008

ISBN 0-632-05584-7

A catalogue record for this title is available from the British Library

Set in 10.5/13.5pt Optima
by DP Photosetting, Aylesbury, Bucks
Printed and bound by Replika Press Pvt. Ltd., India.

The publisher's policy is to use permanent paper from mills that operate a sustainable forestry policy, and which has been manufactured from pulp processed using acid-free and elementary chlorine-free practices. Furthermore, the publisher ensures that the text paper and cover board used have met acceptable environmental accreditation standards.

For further information on Blackwell Publishing, visit our website:
www.blackwellpublishing.com

Contents

Preface

This book explains the reponsibilities of the fashion buyer. It is based partly on my own experience and on interviews undertaken during 2000 and 2001 with buyers working for five different fashion companies, from assistant to managerial level, thereby offering a broad and current perspective on the buying function. Buying can be a more lucrative career than designing at all levels of the fashion market, as a wide range of skills is required to fulfil this demanding role. Buying fashion merchandise differs significantly from buying for other product types, due to the relatively short life cycle of fashion items, the majority of which become obsolete within six months. It is this planned obsolescence which simultaneously boosts sales within the clothing industry through the constant introduction of new products, and constantly challenges buyers and designers to develop innovative and profitable clothing ranges.

At the start of my career in the fashion industry as a trainee buyer, I found myself exposed to new systems and a language with which I was unfamiliar. Having secured this post shortly after graduation, I had no real idea of what the job would entail apart from a perception that I would be responsible for a large amount of the company's money by selecting clothes intended to appeal to customers for specific seasons. At the time, I did not realise that it usually takes some years before a buyer is given this level of responsibility. I wondered why no 'guide to buying' was available to explain the relevant terminology and procedures, as this would have been very helpful to me and my colleagues. The aim of this book, therefore, is to document the information which I would have found useful before embarking on a career in buying. The book also aims to inform those in the field of fashion design about the role of the buyers with whom they regularly work.

Helen Goworek

Acknowledgements

Many people have supported me in writing this book, either by being interviewed or by reading relevant chapters and making useful recommendations. I was very pleased (and a little amazed) to find that every person whom I asked to help agreed to do so, despite the fact that they all have extremely busy jobs within the fashion industry. I would like to thank the following people (in alphabetical order), all of whom have influenced the content of this book: Alison Beattie, Kate Bostock, Johnnie Boden, Sandra Bojko, Sue Coghlan, Fiona Copeland, Steve Cochrane, Vanessa Denza, Christine Gerrard, Caroline Gration, Andrew Grimes, Sasha Heaney, Robin Howard, Beth Jelly, Barbara Kennington, Jo Mould, Sue Myatt, Aimee Read, Nicola O'Reilly, Julia Richards, Anna Smith, Debbie Torr, Kate Wells and Barbara Ziemba. Thanks are also due to Richard Miles for giving me the opportunity to fulfil a long held ambition by commissioning this book, and Alison and Stuart Birtwistle who kindly gave me the computer on which this book was written.

I would like to thank my tutors from the BA(Hons) Fashion Marketing degree at Newcastle Polytechnic (now the University of Northumbria), Vivien Todd, and the late Liz Ford, who encouraged and inspired me to work within the fashion industry and to become involved in fashion design education. I would also like to thank my husband, Dave, for his constant support.

The book is dedicated to my mother and to the memory of Liz Ford, both of whom have been my role models and have had a significant impact on my education and career.

Figure 9.1 is reproduced with kind permission of the Next Directory. Figure 10.2 is reproduced with kind permission of Steve Cochrane.

Glossary of Fashion Buying Terms

Allocators are responsible for allocating specific styles and quantities of merchandise to retail outlets. (Some retailers refer to this role as branch merchandiser.)

Art directors are responsible for designing the layout of a brochure or mail order catalogue, including the co-ordination of photo shoots.

Branded merchandise refers to products which have not been designed or developed in-house by the retailer, and are sold under the brand name of the supplier. This applies mainly to middle-market and designer-level products.

CIF stands for 'carriage, insurance and freight'. It applies to the price charged for a product by a supplier, meaning that the product's price includes delivery and insurance for the goods from the supplier's premises to a specified location (such as a UK port). It is often used with reference to the price per metre of a fabric.

Classics are products which have a long-term appeal to consumers, usually for a period of years.

CMT stands for 'cut, make and trim'. This term is applied to garment manufacturers who do not provide design or pattern cutting facilities, and are purely involved in the cutting and manufacturing processes.

Colour palette refers to a selected group of colours used within a co-ordinating range of products.

Colourway is the term for a colour in which a particular garment is produced. Many fashion garments are sold in more than one colourway to offer the customer a wider choice, thereby maximising sales. Several garments within a co-ordinated range may be produced in the same colourway.

Comparative shopping is research into comparable products available from competing retailers. Buyers and designers usually undertake comparative shopping at least once per season, either for their own reference or to produce reports to share with their colleagues.

Confined prints are fabric prints which are exclusive to a certain retailer for a given period of time.

Cost price is the price charged by a supplier to a retailer for a product.

Copywriters write the product descriptions used in mail order catalogues.

Core product refers to basic garment styles which are available for more than one season. (This term is interchangeable with **classic** product.)

Couture fashion is featured in catwalk shows, designed by couturiers based in Paris. Couture is the most expensive category of fashion merchandise, as it is individually fitted to each customer and garments are hand-sewn.

Critical path is the series of key deadlines for product development and production which must be met in order for a product range to be delivered to stores for a set date.

Customer profile is a visual and/or written description of the type of customer at whom a retailer aims its products.

Diffusion ranges are garments produced by ready-to-wear designers at a cheaper price level than their standard ranges.

Directional shopping refers to trips for fashion designers and buyers to major fashion cities to provide inspiration and fashion concepts for future seasons.

Entry prices are the lowest retail price points within a range of products.

Fabric merchants buy fabric in bulk, enabling them to sell it from stock, in lower quantities than the fabric manufacturer's minimum.

Fabric sourcing refers to the process of contacting fabric suppliers to select fabrics for garment ranges. Buyers, designers and fabric technologists can all be involved in fabric sourcing, which takes place mostly in meetings with sales representatives from fabric suppliers, or at fabric trade fairs.

Fabric technologists are responsible for ensuring that fabrics meet the quality standards required by fashion retailers. Fabric technologists can be employed by retailers, garment manufacturers or independent testing laboratories.

Fads are fashions which are popular for a relatively short period of time, usually no longer than one season.

Final range selection is the meeting at which buyers present samples of their ranges for a particular season to colleagues and management. This is usually the stage at which the range is finalised.

FOB stands for 'free on board'. The term applies to the price charged for a product by a supplier, meaning that the price does not include delivery and insurance for the goods. It is often used with reference to the price per metre of a fabric. The purchaser therefore has to arrange delivery of the goods, or pay an additional charge for the supplier to deliver them.

Garment sourcing refers to liaison between fashion retailers and garment suppliers, with the aim of selecting garments to be sold in retailers' product ranges.

Grades are samples of garment styles in a specified range of sizes, e.g. for womenswear this may include the standard size 12 as well as samples in the smallest and largest sizes which have been ordered.

Lab dye or 'lab dip' is a small swatch of a fabric selected for a garment style, dyed to a specified shade. Lab dyes are usually sent by fabric suppliers to buyers for approval before the fabric is dyed in bulk production.

Lead time is the total duration of time which elapses from placing an order to the delivery of goods. This usually includes production and transportation of the goods.

Mark-up is the difference between the cost price and retail selling price of a product.

Margin is another term for mark-up, and is usually expressed as a percentage of the selling price.

Merchandisers are responsible for ensuring that the products within a range are delivered from suppliers to the retailer in the right quantities at the right time. They work closely with buyers and suppliers to monitor the sales of current ranges and progress of ranges under development. (Merchandisers may be referred to as stock controllers in some companies.)

Minimums are the smallest amounts of products which suppliers can manufacture. It is rarely viable for the suppliers to make less than the specified minimum quantity of a product, due to the costs involved in developing products, unless a premium price is charged.

New line sheets are forms compiled by buyers and merchandisers listing all of the relevant details about an individual product style. The new line sheet is used by the retailer and supplier as the definitive reference document for the style. (Certain retailers have different terms for new line sheets, e.g. purchase orders.)

Open-to-buy is part of the retailer's budget for buying stock, retained for purchases close to or during a particular season, after the majority of the range has been bought.

Overseas sourcing offices are used by fashion retailers to liaise with suppliers in other countries.

Phases are periods within a season, during which new merchandise is introduced to stores. Many fashion retailers develop ranges for at least three phases per season.

Point-of-sale refers to in-store promotional material, e.g. brochures and postcards.

Potential customers are those at whom a retailer aims its products, usually defined by age, life style and income bracket.

Pre-selection is a meeting prior to final range selection, at which buyers, merchandisers and QCs analyse a product range, making amendments to styles and prices where necessary.

Progress chasing involves checking the development of the products within a range, at each stage of the critical path, through liaison between buyers, suppliers, QCs and merchandisers.

PR stands for 'public relations'. Retailers use in-house PR departments or independent PR companies to contact the press to gain editorial coverage of the company's products in magazines and newspapers.

Product life cycle refers to the timescale from the launch of a product through to its decline.

QC stands for 'quality controller', or 'quality control'. Most fashion retailers employ QCs to monitor the quality standards of merchandise, and to ensure that products fit correctly. (Certain retailers refer to this role as QA ('quality assurer') or garment technologist.)

Range plan is a chart containing the finalised details of each product within a range for a particular season.

Range planning involves planning the number and types of products required within a range for a future season, taking into account predicted fashion trends and historical sales information.

Ready-to-wear refers to garments by designers who show their ranges at the seasonal catwalk collections in cities such as London, Paris, Milan or New York. Ready-to-wear ranges are less expensive than couture ranges, as they are not made to fit individual customers, but cost substantially more than mass market garments. (Ready-to-wear is also known by the French term *prêt-à-porter.*)

Repeat orders are made by buyers or merchandisers for styles which are expected to sell out within a relatively short time. If the original supplier does not have sufficient production capacity, the buyer may place the repeat with another manufacturer if the design has been developed by the retailer, a process known as 'copy action'.

Sealing samples are samples of garments selected for a range, which have been finalised and approved for fit. The retailer's QC approves the style by signing a seal which is attached to the garment. Both the retailer and manufacturer retain a sealing sample for each style, to specify the standard which garments must achieve in production.

Spec. sheet is an abbreviation of 'specification sheet'. A spec. sheet is produced by a designer, containing a working drawing and details on garment make-up, fabric and trims, to enable a sample garment to be made.

Strike-off is the term used for the printing of a design onto a sample of fabric. Strike-offs are submitted to buyers for approval of colour before fabric is printed in bulk production.

TYLY stands for 'this year/last year'. This term refers to the current financial performance of a product range in comparison to the previous year, e.g. the amount of sales turnover for the range during a particular week.

Visual merchandising is the layout and presentation of products within retail outlets.

Wearer trials are used to test the durability of garments when worn, before products are delivered to stores. Volunteers are asked to wear and wash the garments for a specified time and the results are analysed by the manufacturer or retailer.

Chapter 1

Introduction

This book focuses on the buying of fashion merchandise, particularly clothing, but the procedures involved apply also to a broader range of merchandise, such as footwear and accessories, since all of these products contribute to creating a total image for the consumer in response to changing trends. The fashion industry is the fifth largest business sector in the UK and buyers play a central role in the development and commercial success of fashion products. Fashion buyers are versatile individuals, combining interpersonal and organisational skills with a knowledge of products and processes. Fashion buying is a challenging role requiring stamina and enthusiasm in order to succeed.

What do fashion buyers do?

This question is answered in some depth within this book. There can be no standard job description for a buyer as the role and title vary between companies. In short, all fashion buyers are responsible for selecting a range of products aimed at a specific market for a specific company, e.g. mass market girls' leisurewear or middle market lingerie. Some of the tasks undertaken by buyers in order to select a range successfully include:

- identifying relevant fashion trends;
- liaising with suppliers of products;
- presenting ranges of selected merchandise to colleagues and management;
- calculating profit margins;
- monitoring sales figures;
- reviewing and analysing competitors' ranges.

It is essential that the buyer is familiar with the type of customers at whom the company's products are aimed as the aim of buying the range is of course to sell the goods profitably. Most buyers start their careers as an assistant or trainee, working in a supportive role for a buyer before being given the responsibility of the tasks listed above. As every retailer operates differently most of a buyer's training is hands-on, and involves shadowing and helping an experienced buyer.

Chapters 8, 9 and 10 contain case studies of buyers from various fashion retailers to give the reader a realistic and current perspective on this important job. No two days are alike for a fashion buyer and activities can vary from inputting data on new styles into a computer to visiting fashion stores in Milan. Administrative duties undoubtedly outnumber those aspects of the role which are perceived as glamorous, which reflects the immense amount of background work which goes into buying fashion products, most of which remains unseen by the consumer. Buyers cannot function in isolation so buying a fashion range is always the result of teamwork, and the buyer is constantly reliant on other departments within the company as well as on an external network of suppliers. The role of the fashion buyer is constantly developing to reflect changes in consumer tastes and the introduction of technology.

Fashion market levels

Mass market fashion chainstores dominate the UK high street, so the majority of fashion buying jobs are within this sector. The owners of smaller independent stores which sell middle-market and designer labels often take on the responsibility of the buying role themselves, or they may employ buyers who have other duties within the store. A significantly higher proportion of womenswear is sold than menswear in the UK with menswear accounting for only one third of the total value of the clothing and footwear market (Mintel Retail Intelligence, 1999). As a result there are more womenswear fashion retailers, and therefore more womenswear fashion buyers, than there are menswear or childrenswear fashion buyers. However there is more competition for womenswear buying jobs and specialising in either menswear or childrenswear can be a good career move. The two main methods of buying fashion products are:

- developing products which are exclusive to a particular retailer or mail order company (sometimes referred to as 'own label'), and
- buying branded fashion merchandise.

The former applies to retail fashion multiples and mail order companies, and the cost of overheads for product development makes this method viable only for large retailers capable of ordering high volume, mainly in the mass market. The latter method is employed mainly by independent stores though it can also be applicable to a lesser extent to fashion multiples – particularly department stores – and mail order companies to supplement their own ranges. Mass market retailers generally have a higher mark-up on their products than stores which sell branded merchandise despite the fact that consumers will pay higher prices for branded goods.

Chapter 2
The Role of the Fashion Buyer

The buying role differs between companies but all fashion buyers are responsible for overseeing the development of a range of products aimed at a specific type of customer and price bracket. There are various levels of seniority within a buying team, ranging from small independent stores, which may have one buyer who also participates in sales and promotion, to a major fashion multiple which has trainee buyers, assistant buyers, buyers and buying managers, headed by a buying director. The job title can also vary, most notably at Marks and Spencer, where buyers are referred to as 'selectors'. Members of a buying team need to be effective communicators as most of their time at work is spent liaising with suppliers or internal departments. Buyers usually buy merchandise for a specific product area. In a small company, this may be a very broad range, e.g. ladies' casualwear, including jackets, tops, skirts and trousers, but in a large multiple, the range is likely to be far more focused, e.g. men's shirts. Usually, the larger the company the narrower the product area will be. It is probable however that a buyer for a very narrow product range in a large company will be responsible for a higher amount of financial turnover, due to large quantities per style, than a buyer for a broader product range working for a smaller retailer. If the range of product categories is large most retailers including Marks and Spencer, Bhs, Next, and George, have separate buying departments or divisions for menswear, womenswear and childrenswear. The responsibility for buying merchandise is subdivided into specific product ranges which may include jerseywear, knitwear, leisurewear, nightwear, swimwear, tailoring, underwear, eveningwear, footwear and accessories. In larger companies roles are usually more strictly defined than in smaller companies where the job may be more diverse in terms of products and responsibilities, calling for versatile buyers with a wide range of skills, as the job can sometimes extend into the creative and technical areas of design and quality control.

The buying role is quite different compared with working for a high street fashion chain store, for small independent retailers and some department stores, as they mostly buy ranges of branded merchandise without the opportunity to become involved in the design or development of the product. The buyer's role is usually different in America as it includes more administrative duties and financial input which in the UK are normally part of the merchandiser's job. In the USA buying is often a subdivision of the merchandising team, whereas in many companies in the UK, buying is perceived as the central role. The experienced buyer's role invariably involves travelling, mainly to see clothing suppliers and to gather trend information (see Chapters 5, 6 and 7). A trainee buyer rarely travels abroad during the first year of employment. This gives a new recruit the chance to see how the head office operates and to assist the buyer before they embark on overseas trips. The first working trip for a trainee or assistant buyer is likely to be to Paris to view the trends at trade fairs and in stores but after two or three years he or she can be travelling to several countries per season, depending on the retailer and the product area.

Qualities of a successful buyer

A fashion buyer needs to be versatile and flexible as the buying schedule may include sitting behind a desk one day writing reports and communicating by phone or email, travelling to Paris to identify forthcoming trends the next week, then flying to the Far East the following month, to meet and negotiate with suppliers. A good buyer needs stamina but should also be enthusiastic, conscientious, professional, decisive, numerate, creative, imaginative and well-motivated. To succeed in this career buyers need to have foresight and develop skills in people management and time management. It is rare to find someone with an equal balance between these qualities and skills and many buyers will excel in some while being only adequate in others. Although this list appears to be daunting, most of the skills are learnt within the job. Enthusiasm and self-motivation are possibly the most important elements as they cannot be taught; they are the main qualities that, together with experience or qualifications will help the buyer to obtain that all-important first job. It is very difficult to ascertain solely from CVs and interviews whether or not a person has the right qualities to be a buyer as most of these will only be developed by exposure to the fashion buying environment. If, however, you already have most of these qualities and the willingness to acquire the rest, you have the potential to be a successful buyer. Even with extensive skills and experience a buyer who is new to a company will require a certain period of training and readjustment to become familiar with different systems and terminology. Companies that do not recognise and plan for this factor could lower their profits as a result when the new buyer's range is launched.

Liaising with suppliers

Buyers liaise with garment suppliers on a regular, often daily, basis. A buyer may spend more time speaking to a representative from one of the company's manufacturers, probably from the design or sales department, than to another buyer from the same office. It is important therefore to establish strong working relationships with suppliers as a mutually supportive approach will be beneficial to both parties. The buyers interviewed for this book each stressed their reliance on suppliers to enable ranges to be bought successfully. Occasionally buyers appear to view themselves as being on the 'opposite side' to suppliers – in a superior position – as they have the ultimate decision-making power. However this can be detrimental to buying a successful range as the supplier may be reluctant to offer new ideas if the buyer is too autocratic. It should be remembered that retailers and manufacturers both have the same main aim; to sell as many garments as possible by meeting customers' requirements. To liaise effectively both the buyer and supplier need to form a relationship based on integrity, reliability and respect. Buyers can only expect to see samples and costings delivered on time by the manufacturer if they in their turn respond quickly and professionally to the supplier's phone calls or emails.

One of the major aspects of the buyer's role in dealing with suppliers is to negotiate prices and delivery dates. The garment manufacturer's sales executive, or occasionally the senior designer, will submit a 'cost price' for a garment, which has been based on the result of a costing process in the factory (see Chapter 7). This may take place in a face-to-face discussion, or in writing. The buyer calculates how much the garment needs to be sold for in the store to achieve the retailer's 'mark-up', which is the difference between the manufacturer's cost price and the selling price. The cost price is usually multiplied by three to calculate the retail selling price, including Value Added Tax (VAT) in the UK (see Chapter 5). It may appear from this mark-up that retailers make a great deal of profit, but their slice of the selling price has to be substantial in order to cover overheads such as store rents, utility bills, shop assistants' wages and head office costs, including the buyer's salary, and – it is hoped – some net profit for the company. The buyer probably has an idea of how much the consumer will expect to pay for the garment and therefore will have calculated an optimum cost price. Initially the supplier approaches the price from a different angle to the buyer, working on how much the garment will cost the supplier to produce. An experienced salesperson working for a manufacturer is also able to anticipate how much the buyer expects to pay. The buyer will obviously want to pay as little as possible for the product whereas the salesperson will want to sell it for as much as possible, since both are aiming to make profits for their respective companies. The buyer and salesperson will both need to be realistic, however, and use their judgement as to which prices are reasonable. If the buyer cannot achieve the retailer's target margin the buying manager will probably need to give permission for the garment to be purchased at this price, otherwise the style may be dropped from the range.

Liaising with internal departments

Fashion buyers liaise regularly with colleagues from other departments at head office, as the successful development and retailing of a fashion range is a team effort, requiring a variety of specialist input. Although buyers will usually be based alongside and interact frequently with other members of the buying team it is likely that they will spend more working time in contact with other internal departments, as shown in Figure 2.1. Of course this will vary from one company to another as not all retailers have in-house design teams, fabric technologists or packaging teams. Buying is seen as a crucial and central role at head office, as the buyer makes key decisions about the products sold by the company and the job therefore involves liaison with most of the retailer's internal departments. The buyer may liaise frequently, on a daily or weekly basis, with key departments such as merchandising and quality control (QC), or intermittently with other departments, such as marketing.

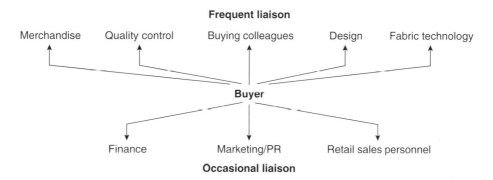

Figure 2.1   Buyer liaison with internal departments.

The buying team

Buyers need to work closely with the rest of their buying colleagues, as their ranges need to be sold alongside each other in the same stores, and are likely to be purchased to be worn together. Buyers from different areas therefore need to liaise regularly to keep in touch with developments in ranges and to support each other. Most buying teams have regular, perhaps weekly, meetings under the guidance of a buying manager. Some buyers may meet more often on an informal basis to update each other on ranges, and to ask for advice or opinions. If there is a quality problem with a garment in the range and the buyer does not wish to reject it, another experienced buyer's opinion may be sought to help the decision making process. Buyers usually travel together on directional shopping and buying trips and can therefore consult each other for advice on the range at this stage. Buyers for product ranges which are closely linked (e.g. if one is responsible for blouses and another for tailoring) are likely to consult each other frequently, to ensure that the range is well co-ordinated. Sometimes the buyer may need to contact another buyer in a separate division of the company, so a ladies' casualwear buyer who wants to source a certain type of fabric may seek the advice of a casualwear buyer from a menswear retailer within the same store group.

Merchandise department

The fashion buyer needs the commercial flair to buy a range, whilst the merchandiser needs the commercial acumen to enable the range to work successfully. Merchandisers interact very regularly with buyers, and are responsible for setting the financial parameters of a garment range. This can include creating a framework for the buying budget, defining the number of product types and determining the number of lines within a range. In effect merchandisers give buyers a shopping list of products in terms of prices (entry, mid or high) and the length of time which they are expected to be in store. Merchandisers have a major role to play in many of the key meetings and processes within the buying cycle (see Chapter 3). They advise buyers on target margins for the range – which may differ for certain garments depending on the country of origin, the flexibility and lead time of the supplier, and the balance of the margin across the whole range. If a product makes a lower margin than the target which has been set, it may still be approved if other products in the range make a higher margin to compensate for it. This is referred to as 'marrying' margins, and is usually acceptable if the average margin across the whole range equals or exceeds the target.

Merchandisers liaise frequently with buyers and suppliers to place initial and repeat orders. This involves regular meetings with buyers to assess the progress of each style in a range, referred to as progress-chasing, with buyers overseeing most of the product development phase and merchandisers taking over at the production stage. Buyers and merchandisers may have meetings jointly with suppliers either in the UK or overseas. Some retailers have a team of stock controllers, rather than merchandisers, who perform a similar though probably more limited role. In some companies merchandisers, rather than buyers, negotiate the volume of production allocated to the retailer for the season. The role of the merchandiser can also include contact with members of staff in stores, as well as warehousing and distribution. Some retailers also have a team – often known as allocators or branch merchandisers – responsible for co-ordinating the delivery of merchandise from the warehouse to stores. A large part of the merchandiser's role is to monitor sales progress, usually from a weekly sales report. Most fashion stores have electronic point-of-sale (EPOS) systems which instantly deliver sales information from all branches to a central database each time a purchase is made by a customer, enabling merchandisers to access sales figures daily if necessary. Merchandisers take action on the basis of sales figures to order repeat deliveries from manufacturers for bestselling lines while marking down poor sellers. Ultimately merchandisers are responsible for ensuring that the product range selected and developed by the buyer is delivered to stores in the right size ratios and quantities at the right time.

Design department

Most retailers do not have in-house designers, leaving design and development to buyers, in conjunction with clothing manufacturers' design teams. However some of the major store groups in the UK employ their own designers who work closely with buyers on the design direction of the range. The retailer's design team is responsible for identifying trends which are suitable for the store for a particular season and will usually put together mood boards, colour palettes and garment silhouettes (see Chapter 4) to be used by the buying team and by the clothing manufacturers which supply the retailer. This ensures a consistent direction across the whole product range and retailers such as Oasis, Next and Warehouse who operate in this way are often easily identifiable, due to their very cohesive and directional ranges. Buyers brief designers working on the appropriate product area by requesting a new version of last season's successful black trousers, for example, or an innovative new style of top to update the range. The design team usually works within the head office building, overseen by a design manager. Locating the designers together enables them to utilise more effectively resources and equipment, such as computers, magazines and art materials.

Quality control/garment technology department

Various titles can be given for the person responsible for the technical and quality aspects of a garment range. Quality Controller (QC) is one of the most popular terms, as the role involves ensuring that the garments in the buyer's range conform to the quality standard set by the retailer. Most fashion retailers have their own QCs who are based at the head office, and, like buyers, are responsible for specific product areas, such as women's leisurewear or underwear. Sometimes a buyer and QC work together on exactly the same product range, but often the QC is responsible for a larger area of merchandise, and therefore works with more than one buyer. The buyer and QC are likely to be involved together mostly in fitting sessions, which often take place on a weekly basis during key times within the season. Buyers are responsible for finalising the aesthetic aspects of the fit and shape of the garment, such as skirt length and proportion, while QCs are responsible for commenting on the technical aspects including methods of garment manufacture and the balance of the garments. The QC usually documents both the aesthetic and technical feedback from fitting sessions and communicates this information to the manufacturer. After the fit of a product has been finalised in conjunction with the buyer, the QC tends to take over the management of the product through to the production, delivery and packaging, usually only involving the buyer if any issues need to be resolved. The QC is also responsible for ensuring that garments comply with British standards, safety regulations and legislation. QCs require a sound technical knowledge, which they may have gained from experience working for a manufacturer and/or a technically-biased fashion degree, as well as by using effective communication and organisational skills.

Fabric technology department

Only the larger-scale retailers, such as Marks and Spencer employ their own fabric technologists. In most other stores the QC department is responsible for checking the quality of fabrics. Fabric technologists are usually involved in sourcing and developing fabrics with suppliers in conjunction with the buying team and are responsible for ensuring that fabrics that go into production meet the retailer's quality standards. Most fabric technologists have a specialist degree in textile technology. Some retailers have their own laboratories where fabric technologists are responsible for testing fabrics from samples and bulk production but this is extremely rare as laboratories are expensive due to the equipment and space required. Most of the testing for fabrics for the high street is carried out by specialist companies which have been formally approved by the retailer's fabric technology or QC department. Garment manufacturers are usually expected to pay for fabric testing.

Occasionally garment suppliers have their own in-house laboratories which are approved to test fabric to the retailer's standards. This can be more economical for larger companies than the expense of sending every fabric to an independent testing house. Fabric technologists who work for retailers are responsible for checking that the fabric for every garment which goes into production meets the retailer's standards and they may also be responsible for setting those standards. If a fabric is slightly below the required standard after it has been produced and is ready to be made into garments the fabric technologist will probably consult the buyer, as rejecting it could mean that delivery would be delayed for several weeks leaving a gap in the buyer's range. This is a challenging decision for the buyer, who may choose to take the risk that there will be slightly higher garment returns due to imperfections in the fabric, rather than miss out on potential sales. One way of minimising the risk is to have some garments made up in the fabric and to ask a few people to wear them for a certain amount of time (a 'wearer trial') to see how severe the problem is likely to be.

Other departments

The majority of the buyer's internal meetings will be with merchandise, QC and design. Other departments will be in less regular contact with the buying team, some as little as once a season. Most buyers will have some involvement with promoting the range in conjunction with the Marketing or Public Relations (PR) department. Garments which appear in magazines are often initial samples made before the products are manufactured in bulk, and these will need to be ordered from the supplier by the buyer. The buyer may work with the finance department when planning budgets to ensure sufficient money is available and to check exchange rates when buying merchandise from overseas. Some larger retailers have specialist departments to organise the importation of merchandise and they may need to inform the buyer if a problem arises, such as a delivery being delayed in customs. The retailer may have its own legal department or use independent legal advice which the buyer may need to consult, for instance if a competing store appears to have copied the retailer's merchandise. The buyer also needs to liaise with support staff at head office including the reception desk, administrators and catering staff, who should be treated with equal respect as they can all be of help in enabling the buyer's schedule to run smoothly. The buyer may also be required to meet staff from the company's stores to introduce the new range to sales staff. Some retailers have their own offices overseas so they can liaise with garment suppliers in those countries and buyers whose ranges are produced abroad are likely to be in frequent contact with members of staff in these offices.

Management skills

Most buyers have management responsibilities for junior staff such as trainee or assistant buyers and buying administrators. Some companies give training to buyers to prepare them for a management role, but many do not. Buyers are often promoted due to their ability to buy successful, profitable ranges, but this does not mean that they automatically have the skills to manage others. If the company does not offer training, a buyer who has been promoted may wish to gain management knowledge by studying if time allows. There are numerous books about management which can equip buyers with relevant skills relatively quickly and easily. The buyer could also initiate informal management training by arranging to meet more experienced colleagues who can share their experiences and approaches to managing a team. Interviewing potential assistant buyers is often part of the buyer's role, which requires effective planning and preparation skills.

It is important for buyers to draw from their own experiences of being managed at a junior level and to view management from the perspective of their assistants, treating their staff professionally and supportively, as they would expect to be treated. One of the most frequent problems for assistant buyers is being inadequately briefed about buying tasks, since buyers may presume assistants to be more knowledgeable than they actually are and briefing time is limited. The buyer must maintain an approachable attitude, and ensure that sufficient time is devoted to briefing. Although it is difficult to find time in a busy buying department the consequences of not doing so can be that mistakes will be made, and the buyer should be prepared to take responsibility for errors if assistants are not adequately informed. A well-motivated, well-briefed assistant can save the buyer a lot of time by making the job run more smoothly but an assistant who is demoralised by a lack of information will quickly become demotivated and less productive and may eventually resign, causing the buyer to go through the time-consuming and expensive recruitment process again. If an assistant buyer encounters such problems, it is worth telling the buyer assertively but politely that more information is needed, with a brief example of a problem that could have been avoided. The buyer may not even have realised that a problem existed, and a professional buyer will be grateful for the discussion and act upon it. If the buyer does not respond well to this information and poor briefings continue to cause mistakes which are blamed upon the assistant, it may be time for the assistant either to discuss the situation with the personnel department or the buyer's line manager, or to request a transfer to another product area. Buyers should treat all colleagues professionally at whatever level; they should note that most assistants will be in senior positions some day and may be encountered by the buyer in another company at a later stage. One of the most difficult aspects of the transition from buyer to buying manager can be to delegate the hands-on aspects of buying and allow the buyers to be responsible for most of their own decisions on products.

As well as being responsible for managing staff a buyer also manages a range of garments, a budget, resources including space within the buying department, and time. To manage these elements effectively the buyer needs to communicate well with a variety of people. It is important for the buyer to meet with staff on a regular basis and a weekly meeting at a set time with assistant and trainee buyers is usually an effective way to manage. The meetings should take place at a regular time, ideally for one to two hours, in an office where the team will not be interrupted. (Remember that if you stop to take a phone call for half an hour and there are four of you in the meeting, you will have wasted two hours of the team's potential time in total.) Set an agenda for the meeting and keep to it, while still giving the rest of the team the opportunity to bring up relevant issues. If an issue needs to be discussed at length with only one assistant arrange to talk about this later rather than using up the whole team's time in the meeting. Key points for discussion should include a review of events and tasks during the previous week and the anticipated tasks for the coming week. Action points should be noted, with a member of the team being nominated for responsibility for each task. The team should be made to feel able to raise any problems that are hindering their work and the buyer should be responsible for taking steps to alleviate these problems rather than simply considering the team to have a negative approach. In this way complaints can be turned around into positive outcomes if the buyer is willing to listen and act accordingly. It is also essential to put positive items on the agenda, such as good sales figures and successes within the team. Too often we are dismissive of success, and concentrate on problems instead; achievements should be celebrated in order to maintain and boost morale. Try to leave as much time as reasonably possible at the end of the meeting before making other appointments as the meetings may occasionally need to run over time to address issues.

A single meeting is unlikely to be sufficient to deal with all of the issues which arise during the week. The buyer needs to communicate with the team on at least a daily basis. The buyer should ensure that assistants are not afraid to initiate discussions when required. The buyer also needs time in private to plan and organise, and may wish to set aside a period to be undisturbed by the team unless an emergency arises. If the buyer has identified a problem with an assistant's performance this should always be dealt with privately and at a reasonably early stage so that the problem does not worsen. This can be difficult to achieve as many buying offices are open plan but a compromise could be made by having the discussion when there are fewer people than usual in the office, or by booking a meeting room. The buyer should give the assistant clear, attainable objectives to improve performance within a set time. After the stated time the buyer should review the assistant's performance and either offer praise if the situation has improved sufficiently or reset objectives. Sometimes the buyer may be able to solve the problem once the cause has been established, if it is within the workplace, or offer moral support if it is the result of a personal issue. Buyers occasionally receive complaints about how the team operates from members of other head office departments. The buyer should discuss these issues with the team and if necessary invite the complainant to a meeting to discuss the problem openly, with the aim of resolving the situation.

The management methods detailed above may be possible in an ideal situation but the buying environment has many constraints, particularly lack of time. It will not always be possible to be consistently good at both buying and management, but if you take a genuine interest in your staff and appreciate how important their support is to your own success at work, you have the capacity to become an effective manager. Management skills, like buying skills, need to be learned, and should eventually become as natural to you as buying a garment range.

Summary

The role of the buyer is to develop a range of products appropriate for the retailer's market, by:

- liaising regularly with suppliers, in the UK or overseas;
- liaising regularly with internal departments, including other buyers, merchandisers and QCs;
- managing junior staff.

The qualities required of the buyer to fulfil this role include:

- stamina;
- enthusiasm and motivation;
- product knowledge;
- creativity.

Chapter 3
The Buying Cycle

The fashion industry traditionally splits the year into two main seasons: spring/summer (February to July) and autumn/winter (August to January). The competitive and constantly changing fashion business requires a more frequent introduction of merchandise, resulting in most stores introducing new ranges at least every three months. The buying cycle refers to the key events and processes in which the fashion buyer is involved in order to buy a garment range in for a retail or mail order company. Figure 3.1 lists the main events in the buying cycle chronologically. The length of the buying cycle varies between companies but usually takes a year between reviewing the current season's sales and delivering into stores. For example in August a buyer from Next will review the current year's spring/summer sales and begin directional shopping to inspire concepts for the autumn/winter range for the following year.

Although the buying cycle for a whole season's range can take up to a year, it is possible to develop smaller ranges and individual garments more quickly, and most buyers keep between 10 per cent and 25 per cent of the season's budget available (referred to as the 'open-to-buy') to respond to trends by purchasing 'hot' items. For retailers aiming at the more fashion-conscious younger end of the market the whole buying cycle is usually much shorter, in order to respond to trends rapidly. This can sometimes reduce the quality of the merchandise as speed of manufacture may take priority, but being able to buy a current fashion item at a competitive price is probably more important to the target customer. The time taken to make bulk orders of garments can vary greatly but as a rough estimate production of fabric can take about six weeks, and manufacture of a single style may take about four weeks. This is a very simplistic estimate, as there are many other factors which affect the time from order to delivery of products. If the fabric or the garments are made overseas, transport time needs to be built in. The manufacture of each style needs to be planned into a factory's production schedule, and this can result in a gap between arrival of the fabric and the commencement of bulk production.

It is essential to remember that the intended outcome of the buying cycle is that the customer will want to purchase the range, so the requirements of the potential customer must be taken into consideration by the buyer at every stage. The features in brackets in Figure 3.1 are the responsibility only of buyers who become involved in product development and would not be relevant to retailers who buy branded ranges for either department stores or smaller, independent stores. The dates included are for guidance only and will vary between companies. Some of the more basic or classic products within a range may be sold from August to January, with fashion items being available for between one and three months.

Task	Approximate date
Review of current season's sales	early August
↓	
Budget planning	mid-August
↓	
Comparative shopping	August-September
↓	
Directional shopping	August-October
↓	
(Fabric sourcing)	October-December
↓	
Range planning	October-November
↓	
Garment sourcing	November
↓	
(Pre-selection)	early December
↓	
Price negotiation with suppliers	November-December
↓	
Final range selection	mid-December
↓	
Placing orders for ranges	December-January
↓	
(Product development – sample fittings, fabric testing)	January-April
↓	
Bulk garment manufacture	April-July
↓	
Delivery of products to retailer	August
↓	
PURCHASE BY CUSTOMER	August-October

Figure 3.1   An example of the buying cycle for a Phase 1 autumn/winter range.

Though the buying cycle can take up to a year there are obviously two main ranges to be bought annually, so the buyer is always working on at least two seasons' ranges simultaneously. While the buyer is planning a range for the autumn/winter season, garment fittings and approvals of fabric colour and quality are still under way for the spring/summer season. Most fashion buyers now buy ranges more frequently than twice per year as an autumn/winter range has to change in order to meet customers' needs effectively from August to January in terms of both climate and fashionability. It is usual for most UK fashion retailers to introduce new ranges to stores at least once every six weeks. This does not mean completely changing the range, but frequently introducing new fashion items whilst retaining bestsellers and/or basic lines in store. Ranges which bridge the gap between one season and the next are called 'transitional', accounting for the fact that the spring season is actually launched during winter (in February) and the autumn range during summer (August). This makes the fashion buying environment extremely challenging as the workload for two or three seasons' ranges will overlap leaving little time to rest in between.

Review of current season's sales and budget planning

The buyer constantly reviews sales figures, which are available at least once a week, to be aware of how the range is performing. The merchandise department usually takes responsibility for compiling a review of the whole previous season's performance of the range so that the bestsellers and poor sellers (dogs) can be identified. This review often takes the form of a presentation to the buying team (and the design department if the company has one) with samples of garments from the range being shown and analysed. This may be known as a sales review or range direction meeting. Assistant buyers may be asked to help organise the presentation by acquiring relevant garment samples. The QC department may contribute towards the meeting by commenting on any technical problems which may explain low sales figures, for instance the colour or fit in production differing from the catalogue photograph of the garment. Alternatively the QC department may organise a separate presentation to discuss garment quality issues.

After the review of sales figures buyers are armed with the knowledge of which styles the customer currently likes and dislikes; offers a framework of successes to build upon for the new season, and a rough idea of the new range plan can start to be pencilled in. They may also be able to learn from other buyers' sales figures, so if a new fabric or colour has been trialled in another product area the buyer can decide whether or not to run it too. The buyer may instinctively avoid including in the new range a version of a garment which has previously sold poorly but this needs to be viewed within the context of current trends; it is possible that the style was offered too early for the customer, so this type of garment should not be completely dismissed. Low sales could also be caused by low quality standards of fabric or garment manufacture and the buyer may therefore choose to buy a similar style from a different supplier as a result. If a garment has sold particularly well the buyer will probably decide to run one or more versions of this style in the next season.

However the buyer may view the bestseller as a short-term fad and decide not to run it again.

Merchandisers usually plan budgets in conjunction with buyers. The framework for the budget is based largely on the last season's performance as discussed at the range review, as well as any anticipated developments. For example if tailoring is predicted to be a major trend for a future season and dressing casually is considered to have reached the peak of its sales potential, the tailoring budget may be increased and the investment in the leisurewear range reduced accordingly. The buyer should be far more informed about this type of fashion trend than the merchandising or finance departments and therefore needs to utilise this information to influence budget-setting.

Even before design concepts have been developed it is possible to estimate the total value of a range by defining the number of styles with provisional quantities. The merchandise department may construct the price architecture of the range by planning the number of styles per retail selling price. The finance department may also be involved in budget planning as they should be aware of the amount of money that the company has available to purchase future ranges. Assistant buyers are rarely involved in budget planning, as this is one of the managerial roles of buyers and buying managers.

Comparative shopping

Comparative shopping is often referred to as a comp. shop, and is usually undertaken at the beginning of each season by the buying and/or design teams. This means looking at current merchandise in the stores of competitors which sell comparable ranges (similar product types and prices). A report will often be produced after the comp. shop visit, to be distributed amongst the team. This may include some sketches and often takes the form of a grid with descriptions of products compared with prices, fabrics and colours of similar merchandise from competing stores. A conclusion may be added analysing how the competitors' ranges compare with each other and noting any important trends or styles which are missing from the buyer's range so that this may be acted upon quickly. Some stores compile comp. shop reports at least once a month and this can often be one of the first tasks given to trainee buyers to familiarise them with competitors in the same market.

Directional shopping

'Directional shopping' is the term used for trips to gain inspiration for design concepts for a new season. Many buyers visit cities such as Paris, London,

Milan and New York for directional shopping trips, depending on the company's travel budget. The choice of locations to visit also depends on the buyer's product range. Florence and Brussels are popular for childrenswear whereas Paris is appropriate for all types of men's, women's and children's merchandise. During a trip, the buyer visits stores which are more directional than his or her own range, stocking merchandise following trends ahead of the buyer's own company. Most of the stores visited usually stock designer ready-to-wear ranges but buyers may also visit mass market stores which are aimed at a younger market or are more expensive than the buyer's own range as they are also likely to stock influential styles. The buyer makes notes on key shapes, details, colour and fabric for reference, and after visiting several stores a picture will start to emerge of the key trends which are coming through. Buyers are usually given a budget to buy garments during directional shopping trips, and these are referred to as bought samples, which typify the key trends.

Retailers invest a substantial amount of money in directional shopping trips and so the schedule has to be strategically planned beforehand, to maximise the use of time. This involves deciding which areas of the city to visit and allowing time to travel between one area and another. It is often more economical to visit several countries consecutively; a trip to Europe for a childrenswear buyer could include a weekend in Paris followed by a day in Brussels and two days in Florence. Trips always take up some of the buyer's own free time and many visits include weekends for which time off in lieu is unlikely to be given. During a trip the buyer will usually visit the shops as soon as they open and continue working until closing time. Directional shopping is viewed as one of the most exciting aspects of the buyer's role but it can also be one of the most tiring parts of the job. During the evening the buyer is unlikely to be able to rest as this is a time to meet up with colleagues to review the day's work and sometimes provides an opportunity to socialise. Such trips can often be viewed by other colleagues as holidays for the buying team, but it is unfair to make this comparison. Some trips abroad can be as short as one day with the buyer taking an early morning flight and returning to work in the office the next day. In some companies designers may take the responsibility for directional shopping and often buyers and designers will travel together. In the future buyers' directional shopping trips could become more restricted due to the worldwide availability of information on designer ranges on the internet and tighter travel budgets. The subscription fee to a website such as wgsn.com which offers the subscriber access to photographs of designer collections and store windows from around the world can prove to be cheaper and less time-consuming than sending a team of buyers abroad.

Range planning and selection

Range planning is the stage where buyers define the detail of the range that is to be offered to the customer in terms of styling, fabric, design details, suppliers and prices (described in detail in Chapter 5). Many buyers do not become directly involved in fabric sourcing as designers or fabric technologists working for the retailer or for manufacturers may be responsible for this, but the buyer is responsible for the selection of fabric for each garment (see Chapter 6). Some buyers may still choose to visit *Première Vision*, the major international fabric trade fair held in Paris twice annually, to gain an overview of fabric and colour trends. This is often combined with a directional shopping trip to Paris. By definition all fashion buyers are required to source garments. Sometimes the garments are designed by the retailer's in-house design team but more frequently they are produced by designers working for garment manufacturers. Buyers may purchase garments from the supplier's original designs or may develop garments in conjunction with the manufacturer (see Chapter 7). When the buyers have completed the range planning stage, a pre-selection meeting takes place where buyers present garment samples for the range to their buying, merchandise and QC teams. Departmental managers attend this pre-selection meeting to offer a critique on aspects such as styling, colour and price. The overall strategy for the season and supplier base may be discussed within the meeting. Numerous amendments are likely to be made to a range at pre-selection as it is the first opportunity for the buying team to gain an overview of the whole department's products. Buyers must anticipate changes to garments at pre-selection and learn not to take them personally, as the intention of any amendments should be to improve potential sales to customers. Buyers should be prepared to justify all decisions in relation to the garments where necessary and to fight (diplomatically) for the inclusion of those styles which they consider to have the potential to be bestsellers.

The period immediately after pre-selection can be the busiest time of the year as buyers usually have about two weeks to prepare for the most important meeting of the season: final range selection. Most of the work involves contacting suppliers to explain that some garments have been removed from the range, others added, and existing styles amended. Prices may need to be renegotiated if garments have been shortened, fabrics changed or trims removed. New samples may be requested, and the range plan rewritten to include the changes. The final range selection meeting gives buyers the opportunity to present the range in its entirety with product samples for each style. Chasing initial samples from suppliers can make this a stressful though exciting time, and if garments miss the deadline they are very unlikely to be included within the final range. It is rarely possible for all of the samples at the final range selection to be in the correct colour as the fabric needs to be dyed to the retailer's requested colour in bulk production and this cannot be done until the final order has been placed. Garments are usually shown in the correct fabric quality with swatches of colourways attached, and some styles may be shown on models. Final range selection usually takes less time than pre-selection as much of the groundwork has already been done, and it provides an opportunity to sign off some garments and make slight amendments to others. As most high street retailers introduce new ranges at least every three months, selection meetings take place four times or more per year.

After range selection meetings initial orders are sent to suppliers and then contracts for all products within the range are completed. 'New line sheets' (sometimes called purchase sheets) are generated by buyers and merchandisers for each item which has been selected for inclusion in the final range. Details on the new line sheet should include the buyer's signature, the retailer's style reference number, the season, the manufacturer and country of origin, the manufacturer's style reference number, the cost price, retail selling price, yarn or fabric fibre content and construction (weight and/or gauge), size range, colour/s, description, sketch, delivery/shipping date. The new line sheet is signed off by the buying manager if all of the details are approved, and then distributed to other departments within the company including QC, and to the supplier, as a definitive record of the style. If amendments need to be made to the style, for instance cancelling a colourway, this needs to be amended on the new line sheet and dated and signed by the buyer and buying manager.

Critical paths for product development, production and delivery

The schedule of key dates for product development and production is known as the critical path because it is critical that these deadlines are met if the range is to be launched into stores by the intended date. The key dates for the season are usually planned by senior managers such as the buying director and merchandise manager. These dates are communicated to the buying and merchandise teams in order to plan visits and meetings with relevant departments and suppliers. The schedule is usually planned in reverse chronological order, beginning with the launch date of the range and working back to the deadlines necessary to achieve delivery on time. Consistent lateness on the part of the buyer, designer, or manufacturer in developing and approving various aspects of each garment by critical dates would result in garments not being available to customers at the required time and lead to reduced profits for the company. The buyer needs to compile a critical path (see Figure 3.2) for every garment in the range to be able to successfully monitor progress. This includes deadline dates for such factors as testing of the fabric quality at sample and bulk

SEASON: Autumn/winter critical path last updated: 26th March

Style no.	Description	Supplier and country of origin	Lab dye/ strike-off approval	Sample fabric approval	Trim approval	Size 12 fitting sample approval	Grades approval sizes 8, 12, 16	Bulk fabric and trim approval	Bulk production starts	Due in warehouse
AW028	Long sleeve red top	TL Co., Hong Kong	✓ Appd. 24/1	✓ Appd. 22/1	✓ Appd. 25/1	Rejected 23/3 – second sample due 1/4	Due 14/4	Due 23/4	1/5	10/8
AW029	Blue vest	BY Ltd, UK	✓ Appd. 14/2	Rejected 6/2 – new sample due 25/2	✓ Appd. 15/3	✓ Appd. 25/3	Due 30/4	Due 14/5	28/6	10/8

Figure 3.2 Example of a critical path chart for the approval of garment styles.

stage, approval of the colour for fabric, fastenings and trims, and fitting the garment. The buyer should aim to have each of these elements approved prior to the required deadline to allow for any rejections and resubmissions of fabrics, trims or fitting samples. The majority of fitting samples will not be approved first time as the buyer may choose to amend the proportion and styling and the QC will probably alter the fit.

The buyer should be sufficiently familiar with the quality standards of the suppliers to anticipate how long it might take to complete all of the relevant approvals and build in time for the possibility of samples being rejected and resubmitted. However this can be difficult to predict as most styles have never been made in production before with exactly the same fabric, colour and styling details. This makes fashion merchandise notoriously unpredictable in terms of quality as production runs are short-term, usually lasting only a few weeks, as opposed to products in many other industries where merchandise tends to be produced over a much longer period of time, allowing many initial production problems to be eliminated.

Monitoring the critical path of a garment range is one of the major responsibilities of the buyer and also forms a large part of the role of an assistant (or trainee) buyer. Most fashion buyers are responsible for over 100 garment styles within a range, including merchandise for more than one season at a time so it is essential that progress is documented as it would be impossible to rely solely on an individual's memory. Manufacturers need to be notified of all the key dates for approval for each garment within the range. Once a style has been selected the buyer or merchandiser gives it a reference number to ensure easier communication and to avoid errors. Even though suppliers should be aware of dates by which fabric, trim or garment samples should be submitted for approval, buyers or their assistants frequently have to chase progress by contacting manufacturers to check when the samples will be submitted, often because they are late. Buyers therefore need to have good verbal and written communication skills. Skills of diplomacy are also required as the buyer/supplier relationship is mutually beneficial, and a reprimand from the buyer for late delivery of a sample may be inappropriate if the supplier meets deadlines 95 per cent of the time. Buyers need suppliers and *vice versa*, and it is not worth jeopardising the relationship because of an occasional mistake. The buyer or assistant buyer will probably have a weekly meeting with the merchandiser working on the same product range in order to update each other on progress on the critical path. Some stores use computer systems to monitor critical paths, which can be updated as progress is made and accessed via a network which reduces the need for meetings. The buying manager may also request a regular review of the range's progress with the buyer and may be called upon to intervene if problems arise with particular styles or suppliers.

Approval of fabric and trims

After a buyer has selected a garment in a specific fabric to be included within a range, most retailers have stringent procedures to which the buyer and manufacturer must adhere to ensure suitable quality standards. The garment will have been shown at a range presentation made from a sample length of fabric. The garment manufacturer has to have the sample fabric tested at an approved laboratory (see below). The buyer will probably have requested the garment to be dyed to a specific shade from the retailer's colour palette for the relevant season, so the fabric manufacturer will have dyed a swatch of the fabric to this shade. This swatch is known as a lab dye (or lab dip) and is usually sent to the buyer for approval. The buyer looks at the lab dye in a light box (a small booth containing light bulbs usually of the same type as used in the retailer's stores) to demonstrate how the colour will appear to the customer when making a purchase. The lab dye is compared to the original colour swatch to which the buyer requested the fabric to be matched. Each lab dye is given a reference number which is a record of the exact recipe used to achieve the shade (the proportions of dyes which were mixed together) to ensure that the buyer can give approval without needing to return the swatch. The buyer should immediately write the date on the card to which the lab dye is attached and whether it is approved or rejected.

If a lab dye is rejected it is important that the buyer gives feedback to the manufacturer about the nature of the problem; for instance a purple shade may need to have slightly more red added to it to match correctly. It is important that all lab dyes for a particular shade are matched to the original swatch from the colour palette as there will probably be several garments in the store at the same time, possibly from different buyers' ranges, and it is important that the shade is consistent to ensure that garments match each other. One buyer could have a sweatshirt made in fabric from Greece in the same shade of blue as a pair of trousers made in fabric from Korea in another buyer's range. Because of the vast distance between the fabric producers, who are not in contact with each other, the buyers need to be the link which controls the consistency of the colour or sales may be lost due to incorrect matching of shades.

Although it may seem unimportant if a shade of blue is very slightly darker than the original swatch it is essential to correct this as another fabric manufacturer may have produced a lab dye slightly lighter than the original, resulting in garments clashing if these shades are approved to go into mass production. Sometimes the fabric supplier may send the buyer several lab dyes for approval so that the closest one can be selected immediately without the need for resubmission if the first one is rejected. For a printed fabric the buyer may select a colourway from the supplier's range or ask for the colours to be based on the retailer's own colour palette. The manufacturer will send the buyer a 'strike-off' for approval, which is a large swatch of the fabric in the requested colours. Suppliers also send swatches of bulk fabric from production for approval, and the buyer will compare these with the original colour and the approved lab dye before garment production can commence.

Fabric testing

Most fashion retailers require fabrics to be tested to check that the quality meets the company's requirements and to supply appropriate washing instructions with the garment. Large retailers may have in-house fabric quality testing facilities, but most retailers rely either on garment manufacturers' own quality laboratories or use independent testing labs. Such laboratories have full documentation of the retailer's requirements and are audited regularly to ensure adherence to the correct standards and procedures. Tests are carried out on a sample length of fabric to give an indication of its performance prior to bulk production. A sample fabric which does not pass the stated test criteria at this stage is unlikely to go into bulk production unless the fabric manufacturer can supply an improved sample. Alternatively, if the fabric is a 'must-have' product, the buyer may reconsider the criteria and accept that the garment will have to be hand-washed rather than offer the usual machine-washing instructions that the customer expects. After fabric quality testing, washing instructions are issued by the retailer's fabric technology or QC department and these will be incorporated in the garment label. Due to retailers' differing quality specifications the same fabric could have varying washing instructions, with a recommendation for machine wash from one retailer and handwash from another.

Garment fittings

Garments are fitted on a model of the retailer's standard size (usually size 12 for womenswear, size 42 for menswear and age 7/8 for childrenswear). Wherever possible the same model is used each time as the fit may vary on different models and lead to confusion. Some retailers keep their own house models and this used to be standard practice for many fashion companies. Now, with tighter budgets, this tends to be restricted to larger stores which can justify a full-time model. Most retailers now hire freelance models from agencies who are paid at a daily rate. QCs may also use mannequins (life-size padded dummies of the torso) occasionally for fittings, which can either be bought in a standard size or manufactured to the retailer's exact specifications. However, it is obviously essential to see every garment on the body to be able to observe how it looks when worn, as well as checking practicalities such as whether or not it is practical for getting into and for walking around. As manufacturing is increasingly based overseas the comments on fittings need to be extremely clear and usually include helpful diagrams. English may not be the recipient's first language. Sometimes a representative from the garment manufacturer – a designer, garment technologist or pattern-cutter – will be present at the fitting if the manufacturer is based in the same country. This system enables the manufacturer's representative to be actively involved in the fitting and to offer solutions to any problems with the fit. This can minimise the number of fitting sessions before approval of the garment.

Manufacturers make amendments to the pattern and garment after a first-fit session – as the style is rarely approved first time – then submit a second sample for the next fitting session. Once the fit has been approved suppliers are usually requested to submit two identical samples in the correct fabric and the QC is responsible for sealing them by attaching the retailer's seal of approval, with notes on minor amendments required, signed and dated. One sealing sample is returned to the manufacturer before the patterns are produced in the full range of sizes which have been ordered (grades) and the other is retained by the retailer, to compare with production styles at a later stage. Some retailers request a selection of garments in different sizes, usually in the smallest, middle and largest sizes, for fitting sessions.

The main responsibility for further development of the garments is passed on from the buyer to the QC department after fittings have been finalised unless the garment technologist finds a problem on which the buyer's opinion is needed. The QC's responsibilities include checking the quality of garments during production and after delivery. Liaison with the buyer is then usually limited to updating progress on approval of grades and consultation if any problems arise. The QC's role includes travel within the same country and often overseas to observe garments in production. This is known as an 'in-work check', involving looking at merchandise which is either finished or currently being manufactured to check quality standards before the products are delivered to the retailer's warehouse. This helps to ensure that quality is maintained and can save the time and expense of returning low-quality merchandise to the manufacturer. Quality inspections include measuring various dimensions of the garment to ensure that they meet the required specifications and checking the quality of manufacture. Some retailers carry out wearer trials on all garments, but most companies do this only where potential problems are anticipated. The QC is responsible for organising wearer trials by distributing the garments to suitable wearers, gaining feedback, compiling the results and taking appropriate action where required.

It is usually not feasible for the QC to see every style in the range in production because too many styles are being made in a variety of locations. If there has not been an in-work check the manufacturer may be asked to send one or more samples from production directly to the retailer's QC department for approval before delivery. When the production of the garments is complete they are delivered to the retailer's warehouse. QCs will often travel from head office to the warehouse (which is usually in a separate location) to check the quality of stock which has been delivered prior to its delivery to stores. Staff responsible for checking quality may also be employed in the retailer's ware-house, liaising with the QC department at head office. Normally garments are checked at random, and as few as one garment in every hundred will be inspected. However, some garments may need 100 per cent inspection at the warehouse, if for example the supplier has had quality problems. If the quality is below standard the whole delivery could be rejected and returned to the supplier, or the buyer could be consulted to see whether or not they consider the problem to be sufficiently serious to end up being short of stock in the stores. A good QC can be an asset to the buyer, helping to eliminate potential production problems before they arise, by anticipating them at an early stage. It is important that the buyer should consider advice from the QC department carefully and take this into account when making decisions relating to the development and fit of garments. Once products have been delivered to the retailer's warehouse and approved for quality they are distributed to the stores they have been allocated to by the merchandise team. Buyers then wait in anticipation for the customers' response to the range, and sales figures are reviewed at the commencement of a new buying cycle.

Summary

The buying cycle varies between companies, but usually contains the following main elements:

- review of previous season's sales;
- budget planning;
- range planning;
- garment sourcing;
- range selection;
- garment production;
- delivery to stores.

Chapter 4
Predicting Fashion Trends

The buyer's job involves predicting trends for future seasons, appropriate to the product range and the potential customer. The ability to forecast fashion trends is necessary because garment design, development and production take several months, so product concepts are usually initiated between a year and three months prior to going on sale. The buyer therefore needs to predict what the retailer's customers will want to buy well in advance of the selling period. Fortunately fashion forecasting is not simply guesswork as there are a number of different sources of inspiration for garment trends. The extent to which buyers are involved in fashion forecasting varies, but they will certainly be required to decide which trends are appropriate for their customers as an integral part of selecting a garment range. The buyer is responsible for observing rather than creating trend information from a variety of sources in order to select suitable looks. This information comprises garment types, silhouettes, details, trims, fabric types and colours.

Sources of fashion forecasting information

Buyers can collate forecasting information from many sources and these are described below. The combination of sources of trend information used as inspiration by the buyer will depend on the prediction strategy adopted by the retailer and the potential customer at whom the range is aimed.

Fashion forecasting packages and magazines

Specialist fashion forecasting companies are located in many of the major fashion cities including Paris, Milan, London, New York and Amsterdam. The packages are usually produced as printed and bound publications containing mainly visual information, such as garment sketches of key shapes and details, trend boards, colours and fabrics/yarns. Some of the main companies in this market include *Promostyl*, located in Paris, and Amsterdam-based Nelly Rodi. Fashion forecasting companies employ teams of designers who compile trends inspired mainly by designer-level and street fashion, social and cultural elements such as travel destinations, films and other mass media, as well as retro looks from previous decades. Fashion forecasting packages are published up to 18 months ahead of a season which makes them extremely valuable when trying to predict trends relatively far ahead of production. They are often split into various separate publications with specialisms such as menswear, lingerie or knitwear. The packages are usually published every six months and purchased by annual subscription, either directly from the company or through an agent, many of which currently cost several hundred pounds (sterling). Prices vary depending on how many sections of the fashion forecasting package are bought by a company. Some forecasting companies give presentations to key customers when new packages are introduced, and send updates nearer to the season.

A cheaper option for obtaining fashion forecasting information is to purchase specialist magazines such as *International Textiles* and *Textile View*. These publications focus primarily on fabrics and colour, but also include styling information. They are published monthly and currently cost around £15 to £30 from agents or can be bought from news-stands in some of the major fashion-orientated cities. Forecasts from this type of magazine tend to be closer to the season and far less detailed than fashion forecasting packages, but they offer trend information within a suitable timescale for most buyers. Fashion trade magazines such as *Drapers Record* (UK) also contain fashion forecasting information, often in the form of reports from trade fairs. The internet is a medium which is becoming increasingly important for the distribution of fashion forecasting. Its immediacy in offering information to the customer gives it an advantage over printed publications which take longer to publish. In 1998 *Worth Global Style Network* launched a subscription-only website (wgsn.com) offering a range of fashion predictions including menswear, womenswear, childrenswear, intimate apparel and knitwear (see Figure 4.1). As well as predicting trends the wgsn website contains a variety of useful information for the fashion buyer including a directory of manufacturers, maps of stores in fashion districts around the world, and extensive coverage of designer collections which goes on-line within days of the runway shows.

Fashion trade fairs

Trade fairs usually take place every six months, covering specialist areas of the fashion industry. Buyers visit those events which are most relevant to their product area and potential market. The most significant international fashion trade fair for fabrics is *Première Vision* (PV) which is held in Paris in March and October each year. Hundreds of fabric manufacturers and agents exhibit their latest ranges on individual stands at this enormous exhibition. There is also a

Figure 4.1 Forecasting page from wgsn.com.

central trend area where predicted colour palettes are displayed alongside examples of relevant fabrics from some of the exhibitors. An audio-visual presentation illustrates the moods of the predicted fashion trends. The Indigo section of the exhibition includes print companies selling their new ranges of designs. Many retailers and manufacturers use a visit to PV as the starting point for developing a new season's range, as the March exhibition includes fabrics for the following spring/summer and the next year's autumn/winter fabric collections are shown in October. PV usually takes place from Friday to Monday, resulting in many buyers spending a working weekend in Paris.

There are many specialist trade fairs for different market sectors, including *La Salon de la Lingerie* for underwear ranges and *Interfilière* for underwear fabrics. In January these two complementary shows take place at the same time and location in Paris as the menswear exhibition SEHM and the childrenswear show *Mode Enfantine*. Yarn shows such as *Pitti Filati* (which is based in Florence and is aimed at the knitwear industry) tend to take place earlier than fabric or clothing trade fairs as yarn is the first item to be manufactured in the chain of garment production.

There are many shows specialising in womenswear, as this is the biggest fashion market sector, based on age group, life style and price bracket. In the UK, designer ranges are shown on the runway and at an exhibition during London Fashion Week; middle-market classic women's wear is shown at Premier Collections; and street style for the younger market is exhibited at 40° at ExCeL in London. Trade fairs are usually open only to people in the fashion trade, such as buyers, designers and salespeople, but some also admit students. Tickets may be free with an invitation from an exhibitor but an admission charge is often made at the entrance. Trade magazines will usually list where and when trade fairs take place; for example *Drapers Record* publishes a calendar of forthcoming international fashion events.

Designer collections

Buyers for stores which stock ready-to-wear collections such as Bloomingdales in New York and Harvey Nichols in London will be invited to have seats at the runway shows in Milan, Paris, New York and London, as they are amongst the major customers for these ranges. Mass market buyers are not usually admitted to these shows but can find out what has been shown prior to the garments going into the stores via several sources. Photographs from the runway shows are featured extensively in publications such as *Collections*, with more limited coverage in women's fashion magazines such as *Vogue, Marie-Claire* and *Elle*, shortly before the garments go into stores. Websites such as firstview.com and wgsn.com also show images from the runway shows. Many buyers travel to the major fashion cities for inspiration, often accompanied by their colleagues within the buying team and designers, either from their own retailers or from their major garment suppliers. Some of the main fashion department stores and fashion districts which buyers are likely to visit are listed in Table 4.1.

The buying cycle is to a certain extent led by the fashion calendar established by the designer catwalk collections. Although all price-levels of the fashion industry employ designers, in general usage the term designer refers to the most expensive end of the market. The designer ranges show catwalk collections twice annually and are divided into two major categories: *couture* and *prêt-à-porter* (ready-to-wear). Mass market buyers are not invited to attend the *couture* shows, as the garments are sold directly to the customers through the *couture* houses. The *couture* ranges developed in the late nineteenth and early twentieth centuries, hitting the peak of their influence in the 1950s. However by the

Table 4.1   Fashion department stores and fashion districts in major cities.

City	Fashion department stores	Fashion districts
London	Harrods, Harvey Nichols, Liberty, Selfridges	Bond Street Brompton Road, Notting Hill Gate
Milan	La Rinascente	Via della Spiga, Via Montenapoleone
New York	Macy's, Bloomingdales, Henri Bendel	Manhattan
Paris	Galeries Lafayette, Au Printemps, Bon Marché	Rive Gauche (Left Bank), Rue du Sèvres

end of the twentieth century their influence had declined and they are now rarely the source of widespread fashion trends, as ready-to-wear shows now have a much greater effect on fashion. The bi-annual fashion shows for autumn/winter and spring/summer retain the structure of two seasons per year throughout the industry despite the fact that high street retailers change their ranges more frequently.

Couture *fashion shows*

The term *couture* is sometimes mistakenly used as a catch-all term to describe all designer ranges but in its strictest definition *couture* ranges are limited to designers with an atelier (studio) based in Paris. True *couture* garments are one-offs in that they are fitted to the customer's own measurements and sewn by hand. Though several customers may own the same style of garment there is a very exclusive clientele for this type of product, limited to a few hundred people world-wide. The price of *couture* garments is often in excess of £10,000 per outfit. Although this may seem exorbitant to the mass-market fashion consumer many *couture* houses, perhaps surprisingly, fail to make a profit. This is not generally due to poor business practice as the *couture* range is the key component in the brand's promotional strategy. The laborious nature of personalised fitting and pattern amendment, expensive fabrics and trims, contribute greatly to the high price of *couture* garments. However the most significant cost is the catwalk show, which may last for only an hour, but can cost more than £100,000. Supermodels parade *couture* garments to a hand-picked audience of press and customers. The costs of the fashion show can be recouped by extensive national and international press coverage which may be worth much more than spending the equivalent money on advertising. This is the conduit by which the general public, most of whom would never dream of purchasing a *couture* garment, buy into this glamorous world by purchasing spin-off products such as perfume. Licensed products, particularly accessories and toiletries, provide the bread and butter turnover of many *couture* houses, due to world-wide mass market sales. Most *couture* houses also have their own *prêt-à-porter* ranges to which the *couture* range gives added prestige.

Ready-to-wear fashion shows

Ready-to-wear refers to garments at designer level which are mass-produced, rather than fitted to the individual customer. Ready-to-wear ranges are shown separately from *couture* ranges in February and September each year, approximately six months in advance of garments being delivered to stores, with most publicity given to shows in Milan, Paris, London and New York. Ready-to-wear collections are less expensive than *couture* ranges as they are not individually fitted, but the costs of staging fashion shows, advertising and the high quality of design, pattern-cutting, fabric and manufacture result in the garments costing more than high street products. The fact that ready-to-wear garments are usually manufactured in smaller quantities than mass-market products also contributes towards the higher price bracket as this can reduce cost-effectiveness in production. However those designers who are very successful commercially and are known internationally, such as Calvin Klein, Donna Karan and Prada can produce garments in equivalent quantities to high street retailers. It is an open secret that most high street retailers derive much of their inspiration from ready-to-wear collections. Though mass market buyers are unlikely to be able to gain access to the runway shows the ranges can be viewed prior to the season via the internet and magazines, allowing high street retailers to develop their own versions of key catwalk trends – often within the same season.

Designer diffusion ranges for the high street

Many ready-to-wear brands produce what are called 'diffusion' ranges, where their signature looks are applied to a cheaper version of the catwalk collections, such as DKNY (Donna Karan), CK (Calvin Klein) and Versus (Versace). These ranges can be very profitable, trading on the status and image conveyed by the brands' more expensive collections. During the 1990s, the diffusion system was extended by several British designers by producing collections in conjunction with major high street retailers and mail order companies. Marks and Spencer were at the forefront of this approach by employing designers such as Paul Smith and Betty Jackson as design consultants. Debenhams have since taken the lead, introducing ranges that are much lower in price with higher quantities than at designer level, but more expensive than the average in-house Debenhams range, including Pearce II Fionda and J by Jasper Conran. Several Arcadia group stores sell their own designer diffusion ranges, such as Whistles Express at Dorothy Perkins, and French and Teague at Evans. The advantages to the designers are that their work reaches a much wider audience and their fees help to finance their catwalk collections. Perhaps surprisingly, the use of such renowned designers by Marks and Spencer was not publicised initially – until the practice became widespread in other retailers – and 1999 saw the launch of the Autograph range, a higher price bracket collection sold in the designer-style section of a limited number of stores.

In-house design departments

Some retailers have their own design departments based at head office located near the buying department. Most retailers' design departments concentrate on compiling trend boards (also known as mood boards or storyboards), colour palettes and styling ideas for future seasons, having analysed trend forecasting information. Designers often travel with their counterparts from the buying department on directional shopping trips and visits to trade fairs, to discuss trends and design concepts at the initial planning stage. Designers for some retailers, such as Marks and Spencer, focus almost entirely on fashion forecasting and then brief designers from their manufacturers on the major trends which they have identified. Design departments in several other retailers (including Adams, Next, Oasis and Warehouse) are responsible for designing the garments which are sold in their stores.

Garment suppliers' design departments

Some retailers rely on garment suppliers for information on fashion trends. The manufacturer's design department will be responsible for compiling trend information and suggesting garment concepts to buyers. The manufacturer's designers may compile storyboards with general trends applicable to the season to be shown to several retailers, or put together storyboards aimed at individual retailers. The design department would probably choose to show the same trend information to several retailers if their customers were in a similar age and price bracket. The design department may compile the trend boards as a team, benefiting from a wider range of ideas and research, or individual designers may work on storyboards aimed solely at the retailers for which they design. A meeting would be arranged between the buyer and at least one of the designers for the garment supplier to present the storyboards, usually in the buying office, or occasionally at the supplier's premises. The manufacturer's head designer may attend this key meeting to support the designer. Having seen trend presentations from various garment suppliers the buyer will be able to form a viewpoint on the main trends which are applicable to the season and the customer.

Compiling fashion forecasting information

The various looks for a season can be shown on trend boards, which usually take the form of a professionally presented collage, filled mainly with photographs from current fashion magazines (see Figure 4.2). A great deal of thought and analysis goes into compiling a successful trend board and many images will be rejected before reaching the final selection. The number of themes required will probably be similar from one season to the next, so for women-swear five themes may be needed, including three new fashion trends and two classic looks. Five themes may have been selected to relate to the amount of space available in most of the retailer's stores. The fashion industry seems to have an unofficial rule that for each season there will be at least one retro and one ethnic look, and the two can often be combined. Although this may seem limiting it actually offers endless scope considering the number of historical periods and ethnic cultures from which the designer and buyer can draw inspiration.

During the late 1990s, fashion trends were highly influenced by the 1970s and Indian-style fabrics and trims. Retro looks are usually derived from at least two decades ago, so the early 1980s look which started to influence ready-to-wear fashion designers in the late 1990s will continue to be one of the main inspirations for the mass market at the beginning of the twenty-first century. Retro looks are rarely revived in exactly the same form as the original inspiration, partly because of contemporary technical innovations, such as fabric construction and new machinery. One of the reasons for a look being revived about 20 years later is that teenagers, who are usually at the forefront of new trends, are not old enough to remember this style of clothing from the first time. As their parents probably no longer wear this look it is a subtle form of rebellion to project an image that has been discarded by an older generation. However as fashion consumers crave more products and the internet speeds up visual communication of trends and retailers become increasingly competitive it is likely that fashions will be revived with increasing frequency.

Presenting trend boards

A huge amount of information is available in the fashion media and the designer or buyer needs to be able to filter out those trends which are irrelevant to the customer, while focusing on those which have the highest sales potential. After observing trends on trips and in magazines, the designer will have an idea

Figure 4.2   Trend board from Adams Childrenswear.

of working titles and the mood for the looks which are appropriate for the season. A brief written description may be compiled at this stage which can include colours, types of fabric or yarn, print ideas, garment types, silhouettes, styling details and the source of inspiration for a particular mood, such as 1950s sportswear. Images relating to these themes are collected mostly in the form of 'tear sheets' (pages torn from fashion magazines). Since many designers have access to the same fashion magazines it is also worth looking at non-fashion publications for inspiration, such as gardening, film, travel and interiors magazines, especially for colour stories, to make trend boards appear a little more original. This can improve the aesthetic appeal of the trend boards, with more variety than the ubiquitous runway poses and may therefore be more memorable to the buyers and designers who use the boards for inspiration.

Having initially collected numerous tear sheets for each story the designer goes through a selection process, being ruthless enough to discard those images which are not essential and possibly needing to seek better visuals for some of the boards. The layout of the boards which are usually A2 or A3 size needs to be considered simultaneously with the content and it is important to experiment with the location of the images to ensure that there is a focal point. It is advisable not to stick down the pictures until the whole trend board has been finalised or even until all of the boards are ready as images tend to be moved from one board to another where appropriate. Fabric swatches which are relevant to the theme can be included in trend boards (although it is not always possible to find them in appropriate colours).

If fabric is included it is obviously important to consider its position in the layout either as a section containing fabrics only or as swatches dispersed across the board. It is important to present the fabrics neatly and professionally otherwise they may not sit well with the rest of the trend information. A title for each theme should be added to the board, so that each look can be referred to more easily. This is usually for the designers' and buyers' reference but may also be used to brief shop staff and can eventually find its way to the customer, for instance as a title for a section in a mail order catalogue. It is important that the title is brief and descriptive to be effective, usually three words at most.

Compiling colour palettes

A colour palette (or colour story) is a selected group of shades which are linked together to form part of a particular fashion trend. Trend boards usually contain colour palettes so that it is obvious which colours are appropriate for each theme. The colours are usually compiled either from fabric swatches or from a computer-aided design (CAD) package. The colour palettes also need to be available separately from the boards, so that they can be distributed to fabric and garment suppliers to specify colours for mass production. Colour palettes made from fabric swatches have the advantage of being easier for matching dyes, since the colour should look reasonably similar on another fabric. For colour palettes it is best to use fabrics with a fairly matt appearance and avoid fabrics with a high sheen such as satin, since the colour will vary a great deal according to the lighting conditions. (However, the reverse side of a satin fabric is usually matt and can be used successfully.) It is essential to give suppliers sufficiently large swatches as it would be difficult to dye a colour effectively from a piece of fabric the size of a postage stamp (though this has actually been known to happen). A garment manufacturer may need to request fabric to be dyed to the same shade from three different fabric suppliers as well as retaining a swatch for their own reference. For this reason it is worth the buyer ordering a sample length of at least a metre of a fabric being used in a colour palette, if the original fabric colour came from a header card from a fabric manufacturer's range. Yarns can also be included in colour palettes, particularly for knitwear ranges.

Summary

Fashion buyers are responsible for identifying future fashion trends from a variety of sources which can include:

- fashion forecasting publications and websites;
- fashion trade fairs;
- ready-to-wear collections;
- design teams.

Trend boards may occasionally be produced by buying-teams but are more often the responsibility of the retailers' or manufacturers' design teams.

Chapter 5
Range Planning

Range planning involves compiling a commercially acceptable collection of garments within financial and design parameters, prior to production and delivery. The initial range plan usually takes the form of a list of appropriate garments that the buyer intends to purchase for a given season and which should cost no more than a set budget. Most stores categorise their products as 'fashion', 'basic' and 'classic' items, though they may use different terminology, such as 'contemporary' or 'core' styles. The buyer should research the following before planning a range:

- historical sales figures;
- fashion forecasting;
- directional shopping;
- comparative shopping.

The range plan is a working document which is presented at pre-selection and final range selection meetings. The range plan is updated after the range has been finalised and then becomes a definitive list of the products to be offered for a particular season.

Compiling a range plan

The two main sources of reference for range planning are the retailer's sales figures for previous seasons, and the fashion trends that have been predicted for future seasons. These two factors need to be considered within the context of the retailer's potential customers and are often based upon educated guesswork about which new trends the customers are likely to identify with. The buyer needs to be familiar with the company's size range and most stores have a variable sizing policy, with the buyer needing to decide whether certain garments should be available in smaller and/or larger size ranges. The choice of fabric for a garment and the amount of design detail included within a product greatly influence the cost, and the buyer needs to be aware of how much design content is affordable within a garment in order to keep it within the potential customer's reach. When buying a new season's range the fashion buyer needs to plan the following, some of which will be guided by the merchandise department:

- number of garments to be included in the range;
- proportion of different types of garment to be included (how many tops compared to bottoms, or fashion compared to classic styles);
- specific garment styles to be included;
- fabrics and colourways to be offered in each style;
- cost prices for each style;
- selling prices for each style;
- sizes to be offered across the range and for individual styles;
- which manufacturer to use for each style;
- order quantities per style.

Seasons and phases

As discussed in Chapter 3, new ranges are launched for two main seasons per year. Within the spring/summer and autumn/winter seasons, buyers develop several ranges to be launched at various times and appropriate for the seasonal weather and changes in fashion trends. Because of the relatively early intro-duction of spring collections in most stores – actually during winter – the 'spring season' tends to be a misnomer and the buyer must ensure that the first phase of merchandise is appropriate for colder weather. The changes within a season are usually incremental with small new garment ranges introduced alongside existing stock. Most fashion multiples take delivery of spring/summer collec-tions in January, merchandised separately from sale stock. The new ranges are usually displayed in store windows to notify customers of their arrival and to entice them into the shop.

Ranges launched at different times within the same season are usually referred to as 'phases', with typically three phases per season. For example, Phase 1 autumn/winter could be introduced to stores in mid-August, with Phase 2 being launched at the beginning of October and Phase 3 in mid-November. For most retailers, the period from late December to mid-January is usually devoted to sales markdowns. As explained most trend-conscious stores launch new ranges at least every six weeks, resulting in stock being constantly updated and offering customers a very wide choice of products. This also results in the need for continuous range-planning for buyers working in this market sector. Certain product areas have distinct seasonal sales patterns, particularly those suitable for particular weather conditions such as swimwear and overcoats. With at least one overseas holiday per year becoming the norm for most customers and the increasing popularity of long-haul winter-sun holidays some stores may choose to stock a small range of swimwear throughout the year. Despite the widespread use of central heating in the UK which keeps many homes at a constant temperature stores typically sell twice as much nightwear during an autumn/winter season as during a spring/summer season.

Sales history

There is much valuable information available to the buyer from the sales history of previous seasons. Patterns have probably been established of the type of fashion merchandise which the retailer's customers have purchased in the past. This sales information will probably be available within the buying office or from the merchandise department. Bestsellers from recent seasons need to be replaced with new yet equally profitable merchandise. It is important for the buyer to be able to judge how much, and in what ways, a bestselling style should be amended to prolong its appeal in future seasons. If the same style is offered for more than one season sales may be lower as many customers have already bought the garment, but if the style is changed substantially it may lose the appeal which made it a bestseller. The buyer needs to analyse which factors contributed towards its bestselling status – selling price and fabric are likely to be factors which can be reused from one season to the next as opposed to colour and styling which tend to be more transient qualities for fashion items.

Translating a bestselling style into the key colours for the next season and changing the buttons, trims or stitch detail could be appropriate for customers who prefer classic merchandise, the middle price bracket within the mass market.

At the more fashion-conscious end of the market however the customer may expect a radically different range of garments each season with perhaps the only similarity between bestsellers from one season to the next being the price point. It is important to include a suitable proportion of new styles within each season's range whatever the market, as bestselling styles inevitably have a limited life cycle and some innovations will eventually become bestsellers.

If garments have not sold well on the other hand, it is important to establish the reasons for this in order to avoid the same problem arising in future seasons. This is often easier to establish in mail order companies, as customers are requested to give reasons for returns. It is important that retail buyers visit stores to discover reasons for poor garment sales, as sales staff can provide a wealth of information about customer feedback (see Chapter 11). However, not all stores are typical; London's Oxford Street, for example, contains many retailers' flagship stores, but the customer mix is biased towards tourists.

Directional and comparative shopping

During directional shopping trips several key garments are usually bought in a standard size so that they can be fitted on a model back at head office, and some of the measurements may be used for specifications for the retailer's own styles. The samples may also be bought for colour or fabric reference and could end up being cut into swatches for next season's colour palette. Intellectual property laws mean it is illegal to copy someone else's design. However this does take place within the fashion industry and though it often happens without legal repercussions there have been cases where the originators of garment designs have successfully sued companies who have plagiarised their ideas. There is a myth within the industry that it is acceptable to copy a design if a certain number of elements are changed. This, according to Mark Hurley, Director of Intellectual Property at De Montfort University, is untrue. The law of copyright applies automatically to fashion designs but it can be difficult to clarify at which point copyright is infringed by a style which is similar to the original. There can be little doubt however that producing style with the same colour, fabric type, silhouette and design details as another could result in a company being sued.

Options and colourways

The number of garment styles in the range including each colourway on offer is referred to as the number of options (or ways). In the range plan in Table 5.1, for example, there are seven garment styles with a total of twelve options. After initially planning the range the buyer should check it again to avoid duplication in terms of price, colour, style and fabric. If two styles are very similar to each other, for instance two red shirts at the same selling price, this can result in one style taking sales from the other. It is therefore advisable to differentiate styles in order to maximise the amount that customers want to buy. If, however, a red shirt were viewed as the season's must-have garment, it would be beneficial to offer more than one within a range; offering two at different prices in different fabrics could help to increase rather than split sales.

The ratio of tops to bottoms is a key factor in the planning of a succesful range. Generally more tops than bottoms should be offered as tops tend to be cheaper, and therefore the customer is likely to buy more tops than trousers or skirts. It is possible to achieve this by offering tops in a wider variety of colourways than the rest of the range, or by increasing the number of styles of top. When buying ranges of lingerie the opposite approach should be taken as customers usually buy more briefs than bras. The lingerie buyer may choose to include the same number of briefs as bra styles within the range or even buy more bra styles, but the briefs could be offered in packs of three or five pairs.

Table 5.1 Example of a range plan.

*This is the quality reference number.

WOMENSWEAR RANGE PLAN season: *Spring/summer 2002, High Summer* product area: **jerseywear**

Reference number	Product Description	Supplier	Colourways	Fabric Quality	Size Range	Cost Price	Selling Price
SS021	Short-sleeved T-shirt with neck cut-out detail	CG Garments, Greece	Lilac Buttermilk Pistachio	100% cotton honeycomb jersey Q. L348	8–20	£4.52	£15
SS022	Strappy cropped vest	ASLJ Ltd, UK	Lilac Buttermilk	98% cotton 2% lycra single jersey Q. RS2568	8–16	£3.97	£12
SS023	Long-sleeved V-neck top with embroidered trim	SK Garments, Hong Kong	Buttermilk Pistachio	100% cotton needle-out interlock Q.F22	8–20	£6.89	£22
SS024	V-neck cardigan with pocket detail	SK Garments, Hong Kong	Lilac	1 × 1 rib Q. F37	8–20	£8.07	£25
SS025	Lightweight hooded fleece with zip	ASLJ Ltd, UK	Lilac Pistachio	100% polyester fleece Q. V2279	S M L	£8.76	£25
SS026	Mid-calf length skirt with tie fastening	CG Garments, Greece	Lilac	100% cotton interlock Q. M239	8–20	£7.92	£25
SS027	Knee-length skirt with pocket detail	CG Garments, Greece	Lilac	100% cotton interlock Q. M239	8–16	£6.09	£20

Sizing

The selected range of sizes in which garments are available can vary between retailers, and between ranges within a store. The standard size range is 10–16 in the UK. A choice of only four sizes can be restrictive for consumers, and many stores stock from size 8 to 18 with smaller sizes such as 6 considered to be 'petite', and size 20 and over often termed 'outsize'. Whilst petite could be considered a flattering term outsize has negative connotations for many potential customers and should therefore be avoided. The Arcadia Group's Evans chain wisely dropped 'Outsize' from its name during the 1980s and has capitalised on its position as the UK's major retailer focusing on size 16 and above, including ranges by designers such as Sonja Nuttall. Women's figures are notoriously variable, and it is therefore advisable to sell suits as separate items as it is often the case that a woman who wears a size 16 skirt may take a size 14 in a top.

During the late 1990s, several high street stores realised the sales potential of extending their size ranges. A strategy of offering the same clothes as the standard size range in larger and smaller sizes appealed to customers as it stopped them from being marked out as different by being excluded from mainstream trends. Until the mid-1990s many major store chains in the UK preferred not to stock larger sizes, partly because it was viewed as less prestigious but also because ordering more sizes could be more complex and less economical because of higher fabric usage. As fashion retailing becomes increasingly competitive buyers have constantly to seek ways to stay ahead of the field and the decision about which sizes to stock can be a critical factor in the success of a range.

Fashion buyers need to review which sizes to offer in complete garment ranges or individual styles. This decision can be based on an in-depth examination of sales per size for last season's range, giving the buyer sufficient information to decide whether a new garment with a similar fit to a previous one should be offered in the same size range. The buyer may choose to seek advice from the QC department to establish a suitable size range for a garment. The overall range of sizes offered by a retailer will probably be a senior management decision and the buyer will be permitted to select size ranges per garment within these parameters. It is a good idea for the buying manager to oversee the sizing policy of several buyers' ranges as customers will probably choose to put garments from different buyers' ranges within a store together as outfits and offering one range up to size 18 and another up to size 24 under exactly the same label would give out a confusing message (size 22 trousers may have no coordinating top in the same size). Some retailers make a conscious decision to give a different label and image to ranges aimed at particular size ranges, like the 'Précis' petite range at Debenhams.

In the UK, size 12 garments, the industry's accepted standard size for womenswear samples, are shown at the range presentation. Garments are fitted on models to achieve the correct cut and proportion before the style is graded into the full size range. Size 12 is selected as it is usually one of the middle sizes in a range and presents less risk of problems of fit being magnified. A buyer who is a standard size 12 will probably be in demand for fitting sessions, but this unfortunate addition to the workload can be outweighed by the occasional perk of a free sample or wearer trial. For menswear, size 42 is used for standard fittings and, for a childrenswear range from 2–10, size 7–8 is often used for samples. Women's shoes are usually sampled in a size 4, and men's in a size 10.

Sizing may of course vary in measurement from one retailer to another as most consumers will know from experience. This is because there is currently no fashion industry standard for sizing. There are British Standards for sizes based on the measurements of the body but most garments are obviously not required to be skin tight and need to be bigger than the body to allow enough room for the wearer to move comfortably. A retailer's QC department or garment technologists usually set the precise measurements for each garment size, including bust, waist, hips and many more detailed dimensions, such as nape of the neck to the waist and sleeve lengths.

Calculating retail prices

It would probably come as a shock to most high street customers to find that many retailers in the UK charge the customer 2.5 to 3.5 times more than the price the manufacturer charged them for a garment. As mentioned earlier this is not pure profit for the retailer as the vast majority, and sometimes all, of this amount is spent on overheads such as store rents, rates, electricity, head office costs and staffing (including buyers' salaries).

Each company has its own target margin and a set formula for achieving it. Calculating the formula will become second nature to a buyer after a few weeks or months working for a retailer. It is important for fashion buyers to be numerate to a certain level as there is a reasonable amount of mathematics involved in the job, but the same basic calculations tend to be repeated frequently, and it is not necessary to have a deep knowledge of mathematics. The merchandiser's job usually requires a higher level of numeracy than buying, although it is usual for American buyers to have much more involvement with figures than their counterparts in the UK.

The price paid by the retailer to the manufacturer for a garment is known as the 'cost price', which is explained in more detail in Chapter 7. At the final range selection meeting buyers suggest retail selling prices for the garments;

(this is the amount that will be charged for the product in the store based on the cost price from the supplier, the retailer's target mark-up (or margin) and the price that the buyer anticipates the customer will be prepared to pay. If the retailer's target selling price is three times the cost price the buyer generally uses this calculation as the starting point, rounded up to the nearest pound. The buyer has to estimate the price that the customer will be prepared to pay, based on previous experience, whilst gaining a suitable profit margin for the company.

It has become conventional for many stores in the UK to round up prices to the nearest 99 pence. This practice started after decimalisation in the 1970s, with the idea that it appealed psychologically to the customer. Since the 1990s however the trend has been for fashion stores at higher price levels to sell garments priced in exact pounds, possibly because the .99p price tag has become associated with cheapness and the lower end of the market. Where clothing is concerned it is unusual for stores to use prices ending in random figures apart from the occasional .49p or .50p. Marks and Spencer and Next now sell garments rounded up to the nearest pound. Some stores combine both pricing methods, occasionally using the .99p price tag for their cheaper merchandise.

Most buyers calculate the margin based on the following principle:

$$\frac{\text{selling price} - \text{cost price}}{\text{selling price}} \times 100 = \text{margin percentage}$$

The examples below are for a retailer with a mark-up of around three times cost price:

(a) Selling price = £30; cost price = £10

$$\frac{(30 - 10)}{30} \times 100 = 66.67\%$$

(b) Selling price = £45; cost price = £14

$$\frac{(45 - 14)}{45} \times 100 = 68.89\%$$

Margins are usually expressed as percentages rounded up to two decimal places.

Example (a) demonstrates that a mark-up of exactly three times the cost price results in a percentage margin of 66.67%, which would be the retailer's target margin. Example (b) shows that if the cost price is lower than a third of the selling price, then the percentage margin is higher (and therefore more profitable).

Each retailer has their own formula for calculating retail prices, accounting for factors such as Value Added Tax (VAT) in the UK at a rate of 17.5 per cent. The formula for each company is confidential and is likely to be a little more complex than the examples above, but new recruits to the company will obviously be given access to it. Many buyers initially have the formula taped onto a calculator, until they have memorised it. Childrenswear is not eligible for VAT so the formula will vary a little, but as some teenagers' garments have the same dimensions as adult clothing, VAT may have to be included. Larger children's clothes require more material and this, as well as VAT, accounts for the increase in prices in children's garments and footwear in the older age ranges.

The examples in Table 5.2 show how to calculate retail selling prices from cost prices, based on a store which has a mark-up of three times the cost price.

Table 5.2   Setting retail selling prices.

Garment description	Manufacturer's cost price	Cost price × 3	Rounded up/ down to nearest pound	Final retail selling price and margin
(1) Girls' red jersey sweatshirt with embroidered detail	£3.28	£9.84	£10	£12 72.67%
(2) Girl's indigo denim jeans	£8.42	£25.26	£25	£25 66.32%

In example (1) in Table 5.2, the red jersey sweatshirt would meet the company's target profit margin if it were sold at £10, but the buyer has decided that a selling price of £12 is more appropriate, as the embroidered logo makes it more desirable to the customer than a competitor's plain sweatshirt which retails at £9. This selling price has the bonus of giving the retailer a higher profit. In example (2) the buyer has decided to maintain the retail selling price at £25 despite being slightly less than three times the cost price, as this is the same price charged by a direct competitor, and charging £26 could result in customers deciding to shop elsewhere. The buyer would probably have to gain approval from the buying manager for the margin on the jeans as it is slightly below the target. The buying manager would look at this in the context of the whole range, taking into account that the high margin on the red sweatshirt would help to compensate, depending on the quantities ordered for each of the two styles.

In some companies after range planning buyers are expected to calculate the average margin, average selling price and average cost price of the range in order to anticipate the expected margins and consequent profits. The principle of calculating the average margin is relatively simple but it depends on entering data on every style in the range accurately and this demands a great deal of preparation. The average selling price is initially calculated by adding together the selling price of every option in the range and dividing it by the total number of options in the range.

In the range plan shown previously in Table 5.1, there are seven styles with a total of 12 options, accounting for the various colourways. The average selling price can be calculated as follows:

$$(£15 \times 3) + (£12 \times 2) + (£22 \times 2) + £25 + (£25 \times 2) + £25 + £20 =$$
$$£233 \div 12 \text{ options} = £19.42$$

A range plan usually includes a far greater number of styles, and it is therefore important to recheck the figures as mistakes can easily occur. The retailer may have software to calculate this.

The average selling price is further affected by the quantities ordered per style, since a low selling price on a high volume style could have an adverse affect. Average selling prices however are usually calculated at the range selection stage before order quantities are finalised, to assess the overall performance of the range. Buyers at a final range selection meeting may also be asked how the average selling price compares with that of previous seasons, and a distinct increase in average selling price would need to be justified.

This may seem like an exercise more suited to an accountant but it is very much part of planning a financially successful range. By doing this the buyer can identify which garments are not making enough profit margin and has the opportunity to replace such styles before placing orders with manufacturers. This type of calculation would usually be undertaken by buyers at a senior level using a computer program such as a specialist spreadsheet, so is not as daunting or complicated as might first appear.

By calculating the average margin of the range the buyer may be able to include garments which do not appear to be sufficiently profitable but are compensated for by higher margins from other garments.

Classifying fashion merchandise within the range plan

In order to achieve a balanced offer of merchandise within any fashion range the buyer needs to achieve the right mix between classic and fashionable products. Some retailers recognise this by having different buyers for classic and fashionable styles rather than dividing the range by garment types.

Classic, core and basic products

Some retailers retain classic products within a range for more than one season either in exactly the same form or by retaining the styling and amending the colour or fabric. This often applies to menswear and even image-conscious chains like Gap sell basic trouser styles for two or more seasons in classic colours such as stone, while introducing more fashionable colours on a seasonal basis. For womenswear classic products tend to be sold mostly at a mass-market level with stores such as Bhs selling a proportion of classic styles which evolve slightly from year to year alongside shorter-term fashion merchandise.

Lingerie tends to have a longer life cycle than other clothing items with classic styles being produced for several years because underwear is usually concealed, thereby reducing the peer pressure to wear the latest styles and colours. This may not be true however for fashion retailers with a young customer profile, as certain types of underwear such as push-up bras are worn to be seen when socialising.

Even at the younger end of the market there are classic products which vary only slightly in styling from one season to the next including jeans and T-shirts. Classic products tend to achieve their status by combining comfort and practicality with aesthetic appeal, like loafer shoes. Classic products can achieve a relatively long product life cycle (see Chapter 11) lasting several years, compared with most fashion items which would usually be stocked for a maximum of six months. Classic colours usually include black, navy, cream and white, but can vary from one product area or market level to another. For lingerie white is a classic and consistently bestselling colour with white bras outselling every other colour put together in an underwear range. Depending on the retailer, classic products are also be referred to as 'core' or 'basic' merchandise.

Fashion products and fads

Most clothing or footwear products which are considered to be fashionable items are stocked by retailers for one season or for as little as one phase (one to three months). A minority of fashion products go on to become classic items. An item may be stocked as a fashion product by one retailer, yet another store aimed at a younger, more fashion-conscious customer may include a similar garment in its basic range. A fad is a very short-term fashion, but one which achieves high sales figures within that period. Fads tend to be adopted more by younger customers at the cheaper end of the market, the style's popularity often being fuelled by media interest. The item's high profile may have been prompted by press coverage of a celebrity wearing a designer item: for example a photograph of actress Jennifer Aniston wearing a handkerchief-style Armani top prompted a deluge of similar styles in UK high street stores in 1999. The buyer needs to use experience and instinct to identify whether a style is a fad or a longer-term fashion item in order to estimate how long a product should be kept in the range.

Factors which affect the performance of a fashion range

There are numerous factors which affect range planning and the subsequent commercial success of a fashion range. The buyer is usually the main focus for the performance of the range but retailers recognise that it is not possible for an individual to control all of the internal and external factors which have an impact upon range planning and sales figures.

Internal factors

Listed below are some of the internal factors within a retailer which can influence range planning:

- promotion, e.g. TV advertisements or window displays;
- available budget;
- the company's buying policy;
- takeover/acquisition;
- the performance of the company's other departments, e.g. merchandising, QC, sales;
- management decisions;
- restructuring.

The main areas which the buyer can research are: previous sales history; customer profile; current trends; and ranges offered by competitors. Armed with a thorough knowledge of each of these elements, the buyer will have a better opportunity of buying a commercially successful range. The buyer needs to work within the constraints applied by the internal factors listed above and if, for example, the company's available buying budget has been used in another product area a buyer may be unable to make mid-season purchases of the latest fashion items, thus losing potential sales.

Most companies' promotional strategies involve photographing key items to be displayed as in-store advertising or on the cover of a catalogue. This can have a profound effect on the sales of the chosen styles, which needs to be anticipated when specifying order quantities. A retailer's buying policy inevitably affects the success of its ranges so if, for example, buyers are permitted to buy only from certain countries they may miss out on manufacturing techniques and styling details available in other countries. The takeover of a company is also likely to result in a change in the retailer's buying policy.

The way in which the other key departments at head office operate is crucial to the success of a range as the development of fashion products is undoubtedly a team effort. Sales staff also play a key role as they can influence the customer's purchase decision in store. Management decisions can overrule a buyer's plans, but can equally be of great support. The restructuring of a buying team inevitably affects the way in which a range is bought as, for example, merging two product areas under one buyer could potentially be a positive move to give more synergy to the range providing this change is backed up by sufficient support and assistance within the team.

External factors

However effectively the company operates internally many external factors can also contribute to the performance of a range, including:

- current trends;
- economic factors;
- ranges on offer from competitors;
- customer buying decisions;
- supplier performance;
- weather.

If there is a downturn in the economy retailers can expect sales to be less buoyant and sales figures need to be analysed in the context of the performance of the fashion sector as a whole. If competitors introduce innovations in the product area they could take away sales from other retailers. Customer buying decisions are obviously vital to the success of a range and during the interiors and DIY boom of the late 1990s, driven by the proliferation of TV programmes of this genre many consumers chose to direct their disposable income into this area in preference to clothing. The performance of suppliers, particularly in terms of quality and deliveries, clearly has a profound effect on a fashion range, and the buyer's reliance on manufacturers was explained earlier. The weather often has a major impact on sales of fashion items and whilst the buyer can foresee certain changes of temperature throughout the year the UK climate in particular is notoriously unpredictable. Fashion sales can be affected directly by customers purchasing items suitable for the current weather but there can be a more profound effect in extreme conditions, such as the widespread floods during winter 2000, which, combined with the repair of the UK national rail network at the same time, resulted in clothes shopping becoming a low priority if not impractical for many consumers. There is usually very little that the buyer can do to influence external factors such as those listed above but, by remaining aware of the market as a whole as well as social trends, their effects can at least be anticipated.

Summary

Range planning involves specifying the details of a fashion range at least once per season including:

- style, fabric and colour details;
- cost prices and selling prices;
- manufacturers;
- sizes;
- order quantities.

Within the range, products can be classified as fashion or classic merchandise. A variety of internal and external factors affect range planning and the subsequent performance of the range.

Chapter 6
Fabric Sourcing

Fabric sourcing is often part of a buyer's job when a fashion range is developed exclusively for a retailer's own stores. This may be done in association with designers, fabric technologists and garment manufacturers. Some buyers may prefer not to source their own fabrics, relying instead on design teams from garment manufacturers to do this for them. Buyers for independent stores who select from existing garment ranges are not involved in fabric sourcing; this reduces the workload but does not give the buyer the option of selecting fabrics. Buyers for knitwear source yarn rather than fabrics and there are specific trade fairs for yarn suppliers. Buyers are not expected to be technical experts on fabrics but some knowledge of the terminology and appearance of fabrics is very useful as buyers are responsible for investing large sums of the company's money in textiles. Buyers are continually learning about fabrics as the industry is constantly developing innovations and reviving traditional fabrics. It is a good idea for buyers to visit fabric manufacturers to view production if time permits as this gives them an idea of the production constraints.

Fibre content

All fabrics are manufactured from either natural or synthetic fibres. It is important to differentiate between the fibre content and the construction as they are two distinctly separate attributes of a fabric. The fibre content is included on a garment's label stating what the fabric was made from but does not offer any information about how the fabric itself was constructed. A single type of fibre such as cotton can be constructed into many fabric forms, from a lightweight stretch knitted single jersey to a heavyweight woven cloth such as denim.

Natural fibres

Natural fibres are derived directly from either plant or animal sources. Cotton, hemp, linen and ramie are examples of fibres originating from plants whereas wool, angora, cashmere, mohair and silk are derived from animals. Fabrics containing natural fibres are often viewed as more luxurious than synthetics, with the possible exception of cotton, which is the most widely-used natural fibre.

Synthetic fibres

Synthetic fibres are man-made, either from oil and coal derivatives, or regenerated fibres. Oil-based fibres include polyester, polyamide (nylon), acrylic and elastane. Man-made regenerated fibres are created by the chemical treatment of wood pulp, resulting in the development of acetate, tencel and viscose. Elastane fibre (also known by the trade name of Lycra ® from the manufacturer Du Pont) has excellent stretch and recovery properties and is based on polyurethane. Elastane is always combined with other yarns and is never used as a fabric on its own; it can form up to 20 per cent of the total fibre content of a fabric, depending upon the amount of stretch required. A high elastane content, such as 20 per cent, is used mainly in swimwear and performance sportswear, often blended with polyamide or nylon. A smaller percentage, such as 2 per cent, can be used in cotton jersey for underwear to help maintain the garment's shape during and after wear. Elastane usually costs more than the other fibres within a fabric so its inclusion can increase the price but improve the quality.

Fabric construction

Fabrics fall into two main categories of construction, knitted or woven. Knitted fabrics always have stretch properties. Fabrics can either be woven on looms or knitted on warp or weft knitting machines. There are also non-woven fabrics, though these are generally used for interlinings, which are concealed within structured garments. Until recently it has been easy to define the type of construction of a fabric because of the rigidity of woven fabrics. However the introduction of elastane into many woven fabrics gives them the capacity to stretch. To tell whether or not a stretch fabric is woven it is necessary to look closely at the weave and pull the fabric both horizontally and vertically, as the elastane usually only offers stretch in one direction. Despite the extra cost the inclusion of elastane in woven fabrics has been very popular because of the comfort, ease of movement and improved fit which it offers the wearer.

Woven fabrics

Woven fabrics can be identified by the warp threads which run down the length of the cloth and the weft threads which run across the width. There are many variations on woven fabric construction from basic weaves and twills such as denim to more complex weaves such as pique, crêpe and satin. Designs can be woven into fabrics including colour wovens, such as tartans, where alternating yarn colours in the warp and weft creates a pattern, and damasks, where the pattern is self-coloured. It is possible to make a particular type of fabric from a variety of different fibres either individually or blended together. Equally, most fibres can be used in several types of fabric construction. Some fibres lend themselves particularly well to certain fabric constructions many of which have become classic fabrics such as silk satin, to the extent that the fibre and construction can sometimes be confused with each other. Silk is a versatile fibre which can have many different appearances in fabric from shiny satin to the duller sheen of habutai. Satin can also be made in synthetic fibres, such as polyester or viscose which maintain the high sheen qualities of the fabric and can only be differentiated from silk upon close inspection.

Knitted fabrics

Knitted fabrics take the form of interlacing loops of yarn and are often referred to as jersey fabrics. Jersey can be made in a variety of constructions including interlock, rib and piqué. Jersey fabrics have differing amounts of stretch within them depending on the yarn and construction. Knitted fabrics are cut out and sewn together to make jerseywear products. Knitwear, however, is manufactured by knitting panels of garments with finished edges to specific dimensions and sewing together only the seams.

Fabric printing

Printing is one of the most popular methods of decorating fabrics, and can be a very cost-effective way of adding interest to a garment. Most print designs are taken from the fabric manufacturer's own range and are usually designed either by their own in-house textile designers or bought from freelance designers. Print designs can be all-over prints, border prints (down the selvedges of the fabric) or placement prints (designed to be put in a specific location on a garment). When the same print is available in garment ranges from two entirely separate retailers this is because they have been selected from the same fabric manufacturer's range.

A buyer can make a print design exclusive to a particular retailer in two different ways. First, if the buyer can guarantee a large order at an early stage or is a regular customer the fabric manufacturer may agree to 'confine' a print to this retailer, meaning that it will not be offered to anyone else. The agreement to confine a print usually lasts for up to a year, after which time it may become available to other retailers. Buyers also have automatic exclusivity for a print if they provide the fabric manufacturer with the design, either from an in-house team or a freelance designer. In this case the fabric manufacturer has the screens cut for this print and the costs incurred will probably be added to the price of the fabric per metre, sometimes making it more expensive than a fabric in the supplier's own range. As a compromise a buyer can gain a certain level of exclusivity on a print by requesting a particular colourway to be specially produced in an existing print from the fabric manufacturer. This could include several colours matched to the retailer's colour palette to co-ordinate with the rest of the range.

All-over prints

This is the standard way of printing on a fabric. The fabric is printed in repeat, meaning that it is designed in such a way that it appears to be continuous. If you inspect a printed fabric closely you should be able to identify the size of the repeat, which is often rectangular in shape, showing where the design starts and finishes. Some textile designers produce their original designs in repeat but others use CAD software to put a design into repeat. Some printing companies employ people who specialise in doing this. It is possible to use various sizes and types of repeat for prints, including half-drop repeats, as shown in Figure 6.1.

There are several different methods of printing fabrics all over, in terms of the

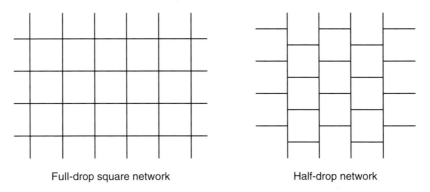

Full-drop square network   Half-drop network

Figure 6.1 Repeat networks for fabric prints.

equipment and dye used. The most popular method is screen printing, usually involving the use of a rotary screen. The design of the print is inscribed on the rotary screen in the form of minute holes, the screen is rolled onto the fabric and ink containing dye of the specified colour is squeezed through. Each colour in a print requires one screen to be made, so the more colours there are in a print the more expensive it usually is, due to the cost of making the screens.

Another method – transfer printing – involves printing a design onto a long roll of paper, and is often used on jersey fabrics. The print is applied at a high temperature and pressure by feeding the fabric and paper through rollers. This is one of the cheapest printing methods but the colours can lack intensity. Transfer printed fabric has the advantage of being relatively quick to produce if the buyer chooses prints and fabrics which are available in stock rather than developing a specific print in the retailer's own colourway.

One-way, two-way and border prints

Some types of print design are more expensive than others due to less economical use of the fabric and therefore higher fabric wastage. Most print designs are two-way, which means that they look the same when viewed from both directions. When a garment is being cut out in a clothing factory each piece can be positioned either way up, allowing as much fabric as possible to be utilised with the minimum of wastage. Some print designs are one-way, meaning that the design can only be viewed from one direction, and all pieces of the garment must be cut in the same direction with less opportunity to fit in pieces economically. Consequently garments made in a one-way printed fabric can be relatively expensive as they use more fabric than a two-way print.

Border prints are similar in most respects to all-over prints in terms of printing methods. When garments are manufactured border prints are usually located at the hem or cuff, so fabric wastage can also be high using this type of design as it is hard to make economical use of every piece of fabric. It is useful for buyers to be aware of this so that they understand why garment manufacturers charge higher prices for garments with a one-way or border print.

Placement prints

As the name suggests, placement prints are placed on a specified area within a garment. This always takes place after fabric production, either directly onto a completed garment or onto a piece of fabric which has been cut out before the garment is manufactured. The advantage of placement printing before garments have been made is that it is easier to transport garment panels to the printer and to place them under the printing screens than print finished garments. Placement printing is particularly popular on T-shirts, and it is possible to keep stock of plain garments and to have placement prints applied relatively quickly.

Fabric dyeing, finishing and embellishment

It is possible to dye fabrics at various stages of production. The most frequent method used is to dye fabric after it has been manufactured to a shade which a buyer has specified for a garment order. Fabric manufacturers often produce fabric in its undyed, unbleached state, which is referred to as 'greige' cloth, to be kept in stock, ready to be dyed when necessary. In yarn-dyed fabrics the yarn is dyed before it is woven or knitted. Yarn-dyed jersey fabrics include *marls*, where the yarn is dyed in shades of the same colour, resulting in a patchy effect on the fabric, and *space dyes*, where the yarn is dyed in various colours giving the fabric consecutive rows of changing shades. It is possible to dye garments after they have been manufactured, depending upon the fibre content. This can cause shrinkage to the fabric and therefore the garment, so the measurements of the garment patterns need to be increased to account for this. Garment dyeing techniques include dip-dyeing, which gives the effect of a graduation of colour, with more intense colour at the hem, fading out towards the top of the garment, or *vice versa*. Tie-dyeing, where parts of the garment are tied up with thread before dyeing and removed afterwards leaves circles or stripes in the original fabric colour, where the thread has resisted the dye.

Finishing techniques are applied after fabrics have been woven or knitted; jersey fabrics can be brushed to give a soft, fluffy texture, and jeans can be stonewashed after they have been manufactured to give an aged appearance. Fabrics or garments can be decorated with embellishments such as embroidery, sequins or beading. Embroidery machines can be used in mass production but beading is often applied by hand, and its labour-intensive nature means it is usually produced in the Far East or India.

Methods of fabric sourcing

Many buyers for fashion multiples see representatives from fabric manufacturers on a regular, often weekly basis, and may spend more time with them than with internal colleagues. It is therefore important to forge positive relationships as both parties have the aim of selling as much of their product as possible by developing products which appeal to the retailer's consumers. Fashion buyers view fabric ranges at a meeting with a sales representative or agent for the fabric company either at the retailer's office, a fabric manufacturer's or agent's showroom or at a trade fair. The buyer will look through a collection of swatches from the fabric manufacturer's range and will select those which are most appropriate for the intended season and garment range. The buyer will order fabric swatches and possibly some sample lengths of fabric. Most fashion designers working for garment manufacturers operate in the same way, selecting fabric swatches which are appropriate for the retailers for whom they design products.

Sales representatives and agents for fabric companies

The people responsible for selling fabric manufacturers' products can be employed as sales representatives directly by the company or can be self-employed, operating as agents. The sales representative is usually paid a salary by the fabric manufacturer plus a small percentage of sales turnover as a bonus. Sales agents usually work on commission only, relying solely on a percentage of the turnover for the fabric they sell for income. The agent therefore has even more sales incentive than someone employed by the company, with less job security but high earning potential, and probably sells ranges from several different fabric suppliers. Fabric companies usually employ sales representatives in their home countries but overseas rely on sales agents who are more familiar with the local market. A sales agent may be responsible for sales within several countries, for example Northern Europe, a single country, or a region within a country. In the UK many fabric sales agents are responsible for either the North or the South, but the North will usually include the Midlands as there is a very high concentration of fashion companies around the London area and it usually requires at least one agent to focus on the South.

Fabric merchants

Another method of selling fabric is via a fabric merchant, many of whom are based in the UK in either London or Manchester. The fabric merchant does not manufacture fabric but imports it in large quantities from fabric suppliers and therefore has the buying power to negotiate discounts. The merchant operates as a middle man by keeping fabric in stock in a warehouse to be purchased by garment manufacturers. The garment supplier can expect to pay more per metre from the fabric merchant than purchasing the fabric directly from the manufacturer but there are usually no minimum order quantities, as the fabric has already been made and it can also be delivered very quickly. This is very important for young fashion garments as it can save three months for fabric production in the Far East, the original source of a high proportion of merchants' cloth. Some fabric merchants specialise in importing base cloths, which can then be printed in the home country for instance by roller printing in a relatively short time to a design of the retailer's choice. In the fast-moving fashion business this is an important service as time can be more important than money in terms of missing out on a major trend.

Alternative methods of fabric sourcing

Sometimes buyers need to source a particular type of fabric during a season, and contact potential fabric suppliers by phone or email, or send swatches in the post for reference. Occasionally it is possible to find the right fabric very quickly, especially if the buyer is very experienced and is familiar with an extensive range of fabric suppliers. However this situation can often be like looking for a needle in a haystack and there are several methods that the buyer can use to speed up the process.

Contacting garment manufacturers can be quicker than contacting fabric suppliers directly as their design teams probably view a wider range of fabrics more frequently than buyers. However this may not be appropriate if the buyer wishes to place the order for the garments in this fabric with a different clothing manufacturer. Colleagues within the buying department should be asked for their advice even if they are not in the same product area, as they may have prior knowledge of the fabric type you wish to source. At trade fairs it is worth investing in a catalogue which lists all of the exhibitors, often classified by fabric types. There is usually a contact in the catalogue for the country in which the retailer is based. Some fabric and trim suppliers have their own websites, so the buyer can source fabrics on the internet. There are also specialist fashion websites with resource directories, such as wgsn.com, which list suppliers of both garment and fabric types. There is great potential in the use of the internet for fabric sourcing in this global industry and the capacity to search worldwide for a fabric without the need for numerous conversations can be very helpful to the busy fashion buyer.

Fabric and yarn trade fairs

The major European fabric exhibitions are *Première Vision* (France) and *Interstoff* (Germany) which are held twice a year, usually in March and October. Yarn fairs such as *Expofil* are aimed primarily at the knitwear trade and take place earlier than fabric fairs as knitwear tends to have a longer product development cycle. Trade fairs offer a centralised colour, yarn and fabric trend area, as well as numerous exhibitors showing their companies' new ranges on individual stands. *Première Vision*, in Paris is such a large exhibition, with hundreds of stands, that visitors need to plan a strategy to be able to target the most relevant fabric ranges. A visit to the central trend area helps the buyer to identify interesting fabrics, which are labelled with the suppliers' names. It is often necessary to make an appointment to view a range on the fabric supplier's stand as there can often be a waiting list, and many buyers organise this in advance of the trip. Sales representatives show buyers and designers new collections of fabrics from which swatches and sample lengths can be ordered.

Because of the volume of visitors to a trade fair it may take a few weeks before the swatches and samples are delivered so buyers may be permitted to cut small pieces of fabric to keep alongside details on price and fabric composition. For this reason it is always advisable to take a pair of scissors, a stapler and some fabric sourcing sheets to a trade fair (see Table 6.1). Few fabric suppliers are likely to have time available at a trade fair to allow students to see ranges, but a visit to the show before graduation can still be beneficial.

Table 6.1   Fabric sourcing sheet.

SUPPLIER			SEASON		Date	
FABRIC REFERENCE Name/ number	SWATCH	PRICE per metre (CIF or FOB) and WIDTH	MINIMUM ORDER QUANTITY	DELIVERY LEAD TIME	SAMPLE QUANTITY ORDERED	

Sampling, minimums and delivery lead times

Fabric manufacturers usually produce fabric to order for customers rather than keeping it in stock as this is more economical. A relatively short production run such as 100 metres is produced initially to make swatches and sample lengths from which to sell the fabric. Swatches are small cuttings of fabric several centimetres wide which are usually attached to a cardboard hanger or 'header', and may include the same print in several different colourways. Headers also provide vital information, such as reference numbers, percentages of fibre content, the supplier's name and suggested washing instructions. The price is not usually included, as this can vary depending on exchange rates and order quantities, and can be negotiable. After a fashion buyer or designer has viewed a fabric range, headers of fabrics which are considered to be suitable for the potential customer are requested. It is important to remember when choosing fabric swatches that the selection must be appropriate for the retailer's customer base rather than being based on the buyer's own taste. Although the swatches are relatively expensive to produce the fabric manufacturer sends them without charge to companies within the fashion industry as this is their prime method of marketing. Charging companies for swatches could deter buyers from using certain fabric suppliers.

Sample lengths are small amounts of fabric ordered by fashion buyers or designers of one to ten metres which can be used to make a sample garment. The garment is often produced by a sample machinist in the manufacturer's design room and can be used in retailers' pre-selection and final range selection meetings. Companies are charged for sample lengths at the same standard price per metre as in bulk production. This is not cost-effective for the fabric manufacturer but once a sample length is ordered there is a strong chance that thousands of metres could be ordered in bulk production. It is also possible to apply a CAD print from computer software directly onto a sample length of fabric using a Stork printer. This can be a very quick method of printing for samples, though the printers are relatively expensive. When viewing fabric ranges, buyers in some companies use forms such as the one in Table 6.1 for reference about fabric swatches and sample lengths which they have ordered. This allows them to keep all the key details mentioned in this section and use as or reminder at a later date, e.g. to chase up delivery of a fabric which is needed for a sample garment. The representative from the fabric supplier also usually keeps a record of the sample order and gives a duplicate copy to the buyer.

When a fabric has been selected for inclusion in a retailer's garment range a bulk order is placed with the fabric supplier, usually by the garment manufacturer, after receiving a garment order from the retailer. The fabric manufacturer has a minimum order quantity below which it is not economically viable to produce the fabric in bulk. Minimums are usually between 300 and 3,000 metres. It is essential to ask the fabric supplier the minimum order quantity when viewing a fabric range as the buyer should know whether this is compatible with the anticipated garment order quantities. Occasionally a fabric supplier may be willing to sell fabric in less than the usual minimum quantity if the company is a very good customer, purchasing high quantities of other fabrics, or an extra charge per metre may be added to make the order financially viable. For printed fabrics the supplier may keep large quantities of base cloths in stock, onto which the print is applied. (The fabric supplier may not be the manufacturer of the base cloth, as it could be more cost-effective to import it.) A minimum order quantity applies to printed cloth as print screens and inks need to be specially developed for each design, and an order becomes worthwhile only if a substantial quantity is ordered. To estimate the amount of fabric required the average fabric usage per garment is calculated (see Chapter 7) and multiplied by the number of garments ordered. Fabric wastage must be included, as well as an allowance for garment rejects, to ensure that there is sufficient fabric to fulfil the total order.

Fabric development

At the beginning of a season buyers look for new ideas when viewing fabric ranges. This does not usually involve totally new concepts as customers are not generally receptive to drastic changes, particularly in the mass market. When sourcing new types of fabric buyers may be looking for exactly the same cloth as the last season but with a different print, or perhaps the same type of fibre as the customer is used to but with a different weave from previous ranges. Developments in new fabrics for the high street tend therefore to be incremental, as the combination of a new mix of fibres, a new weave and a totally new colour palette would probably be too extreme and possibly too expensive for the store's customers. At ready-to-wear designer level, however, it is much more appropriate to introduce fabric innovations, as they serve a different type of customer who is actively seeking something different from the crowd and can afford the extra cost. Those fabrics which become popular at designer level later filter down to the high street, as do garment styles.

The cost of developing new fabrics is generally borne by fabric manufacturers as they continually have to introduce new ideas to keep customers' interested and to compete with other suppliers. Of these new developments most will not become big sellers, but the few that go on to achieve large mass production orders of thousands of metres will compensate for this and offset relatively high development costs. Sometimes buyers find garments on a directional shopping trip, probably from a designer collection, in a fabric which they would like to include in a future range. It is rarely possible to find the original source out of the thousands of fabric manufacturers in the world so the buyer would probably show it to a company which specialises in similar types of fibres and construction to find out whether it was available. Sometimes this can mean sourcing the fabric by cutting up the original garment and sending swatches to several fabric manufacturers. (As this means effectively destroying a garment probably worth hundreds of pounds, swatches are often cut carefully from facings, hems and pockets, since any buyer who loves clothes is reluctant to ruin an expensive garment.) If the fabric is unavailable through the buyer's own sources a company may be asked to develop it specifically for the retailer. In this case the retailer usually needs to be able to buy very large quantities of garments to make the development costs sustainable. This depends also on the amount of development required varying from a slightly different finishing technique to the construction of a new type of weave which would cost substantially more. The fabric could be exclusive to the retailer who has initiated the development for the first season, but would probably be made available to other customers in future seasons to help offset some of the initial development costs.

Liaising with textile designers

Many buyers do not have the opportunity to deal directly with textile designers as they tend to liaise only with sales representatives. Liaising with textile designers, however, can give the buyer a greater say in the development of fabrics and can therefore be beneficial.

Textile designers fall into two main categories, either designing the construction of the fabric, (the weave or knit), or designing prints. Most textile designers work for fabric manufacturers either as full-time employees or on a freelance basis. Buyers rarely come into contact with such designers, sometimes because they are not based in the same country, but it is worthwhile for the buyer to request to meet fabric manufacturers' design teams to gain an understanding of the way in which they operate and to enhance the relationship with the supplier. Textile print designers can also be employed by clothing manufacturers and, to a lesser extent, by fashion retailers.

Some clothing manufacturers and retailers employ print designers to work closely with fashion designers, working mainly on CAD systems to recolour prints or to 'drape' them onto fashion drawings, in order to offer a complete design package of complementary garments and prints to retailers. Buyers may have regular meetings with in-house or garment manufacturers' print designers, to discuss the development of print ideas. Fashion buyers can also work directly with freelance print designers by commissioning print designs or by viewing the print designer's latest collection of artwork and purchasing a print, either at the retailer's head office, or at a trade fair such as Indigo at *Première Vision*.

Fabric imports and exports

Much of the garment production which takes place worldwide uses fabric which has been imported from other countries. The UK was formerly a major producer of textiles but its fabric production is now limited mainly to traditional woollen cloth, such as worsted and tweed, in the North of England and Scotland, and jersey fabrics are knitted in the east Midlands. There are also printers of a variety of knitted and woven cloths in the UK. It is not compulsory in the UK for garment manufacturers to state a garment's country of origin, and even if an item of clothing has a 'Made in UK' label, it is likely that the fabric is from overseas. Garment manufacturers, rather than retailers, are responsible for arranging the importation of fabrics. Many countries are renowned for specialising in certain fabric types and a fashion buyer who focuses on a particular product area, such as jerseywear, will probably work with several fabric and/or clothing manufacturers based in the same country.

Fabric from the Far East and Europe

Certain countries specialise in particular fabrics and most of the fabrics sold within garments in the UK are imported from the Far East and Europe. China produces a wide range of cloths but is mainly known as the world's largest producer of silk in numerous weights and qualities. Japan is arguably the world's leading innovator in synthetic fabrics, including polyester and polyamide, and is renowned for good quality textiles. Korea specialises in synthetic fabrics which are often cheaper, though less innovative, than Japanese cloth. European countries are known more for fabric printing and jersey fabric production than for woven fabrics. France deals mainly with the printing of a variety of natural and synthetic cloths, particularly printed cotton for children's and ladies' wear. Germany, Italy and Portugal are also renowned for printed fabrics, especially on viscose basecloths. Greece and Turkey are mainly producers of jersey fabric, much of which is utilised within their local clothing industries.

Fabric prices

Fashion buyers need to ask suppliers several questions in relation to the price of fabric to discern its true value per metre. It is essential to know the width of the fabric, as it is obviously possible to manufacture more garments from wider fabric. Standard fabric widths are 112 cm and 150 cm, though other variations are sometimes available. It is essential for the buyer to note whether or not the quoted prices include delivery to the manufacturer. The lowest price is 'ex-mill' which means delivery is not included and it is literally just the price of producing the finished fabric. The buyer should either request the cost of delivery of the fabric or ask the clothing manufacturer to arrange for delivery, incorporating this cost within the final garment price. In order to do this the buyer will need to know which country they are expecting to manufacture the garments, possibly even before they have been designed. Prices can also be quoted 'FOB' (free on board) which includes the cost of delivery to a ship at the fabric manufacturer's nearest port. Ideally, the buyer should request a 'CIF' price (sometimes pronounced 'siff') meaning carriage, insurance and freight as this includes delivery to the garment manufacturer's premises and the goods will be insured whilst in transit. CIF prices can also be quoted for delivery to a port near to the manufacturer in which case the garment manufacturer will be responsible for arranging transport of the fabric to the factory.

The 'list price' per metre for fabric, which is initially quoted by the manufacturer, is the maximum price at which it will be sold and is unlikely to be the final price paid by most of the company's established customers. The buyer makes a note of the list price when initially viewing a fabric range, but a lower price can be negotiated if the buyer has a good relationship with the supplier or has a lot of buying power and works for a retailer which buys large quantities of garments. In this case the buyer has a maximum price in mind, for instance £4.10 for a fabric quoted at £4.20 per metre. If the full price is paid the buyer knows that the company's full margin cannot be achieved on the final garment. The buyer may initially offer £4 per metre, knowing that the fabric company's sales representative will probably meet her halfway at £4.10 per metre. Negotiations are rarely this simple in practice but this gives an indication of the typical approach. Sometimes a buyer can negotiate with factors other than price, perhaps by agreeing to pay the list price if the delivery lead time can be reduced from six to four weeks. This factor could be crucial to the profitability of a range by allowing the garments to be available to customers two weeks earlier.

Summary

Fabrics are made from either natural or synthetic fibres (or a mixture of both) and can be of a knitted or woven construction. Fabrics can be treated by dyeing, printing or finishing techniques or embellished after production. Buyers and designers source fabrics by contacting representatives of suppliers and viewing fabric collections, which are updated each season. Many buyers attend the *Première Vision* fabric fair to identify trends and to source fabrics. Most fabrics used in the UK are manufactured overseas, in Europe or the Far East.

Chapter 7
Garment Sourcing

Selecting manufacturers to supply merchandise is a significant responsibility for all fashion buyers. In order to make a suitable decision about which manufacturer to select to produce a certain style the buyer needs to assess many factors including the following:

- reliability and previous performance;
- price;
- production quality;
- speed of production and delivery;
- quality of service, e.g. design and sampling.

Methods of garment sourcing

Methods of garment sourcing vary depending on the company's buying policy. Some stores source garments by more than one method, for example Whistles develop their own garment range as well as offering items from own-label designers.

Selecting garments from manufacturers' existing ranges

This is particularly appropriate for retailers who wish to offer a wide variety of merchandise to several different types of customer such as department stores. It is also appropriate for small independent stores who cannot buy merchandise in sufficient volume to make the development of their own ranges viable. Such ranges usually carry the label of the manufacturer or brand rather than the retailer. Garments can be selected from the manufacturers by visiting a showroom or trade fair, or a sales representative can visit the buyer to present the range. This is usually the most straightforward method of buying fashion merchandise as it involves selecting finalised garments rather than being involved in design and product development decisions.

Product development between buyers and garment manufacturers

This involves the buyer viewing ranges from manufacturers either as garment samples or sketches, and making relevant amendments like changing colours and fabrics, proportions, fit or trims. This method is popular with buyers for many mass market retailers, making the development of the range a joint effort between the buyer and the manufacturer's design department. One advantage of this method is that many manufacturers have valuable sales information about which styles, fabrics and colours are selling well to some of their other retail customers. Sales figures are of course confidential, but the garment manufacturer is able to advise the buyer on which styles could sell well in future seasons. The buyer may also ask the manufacturer's design department to develop ideas based on sketches, magazine cuttings or garments from a directional shopping trip. Product development and production within a clothing factory obviously run concurrently with the retailer's critical path. The processes involved from the manufacturer's perspective are detailed in Figure 7.1 and should be compared to the buying cycle (Figure 3.1) and critical path of the retailer.

Selecting garments to retailers' own specifications

This method gives the retailer tight control over the coordination of a range and is used by those retailers who are considered to be design-led with a strong co-ordinated image for their merchandise. Such retailers usually have in-house design teams and provide garment specification sheets (often abbreviated to 'spec.' sheets), containing detailed written and visual information on styling, design details, fabric and trims, to their suppliers. Retailers who work in this way need to be able to buy relatively large volumes of garments to make the overheads of employing a design team and developing the product worthwhile. The minimum order quantity required to buy merchandise by this method is usually at least 500 pieces per style and many manufacturers, particularly overseas suppliers, require orders of at least 2000 pieces.

Some retailers usually provide the manufacturer with a fully-detailed spec. sheet including a working drawing (a precise technical drawing of a garment), fabric information and trim details. The manufacturer then makes the garment patterns and a sample garment. A length of fabric to make the sample garment is sometimes provided by the retailer, having been selected from a fabric manufacturer's range. Certain retailers take this method of buying a stage further by having the patterns made in-house and passing them to the garment supplier to make a first sample. Manufacturers who operate in this way, focusing solely on garment production without an in-house design team, are known as 'Cut, Make and Trim' (CMT) garment suppliers. (This is similar to the

Product development
Initial design of garment ranges (sketches)
↓
Sample machinist makes samples of chosen designs
↓
Initial sample garments presented to buyer by design/sales team
↓
Selected samples costed and submitted to buyer for pre-selection
↓
Samples amended for retailer's final range presentation
(costings may be amended and renegotiated)
↓
Orders and contracts received from retailer
↓
Fabric, trims and componentry ordered by retailer for bulk production
↓
Samples of fabric, trims and componentry tested in lab
↓
Fitting samples of products in final range submitted to retailer until fit is approved
↓
Graded samples (and/or size chart) submitted to retailer for approval
↓
Sealing samples submitted to retailer – one returned to supplier
↓
Bulk fabric delivered to retailer
↓
Production
Fabric spread and cut in cutting room
↓
Garment pieces bundled and distributed to machinists
↓
Garments manufactured
↓
In-work check from retailer's QC on certain garment styles
↓
Garments finished and pressed
↓
Garments bagged and stored in warehouse
↓
Garments delivered to retailer's warehouse

Figure 7.1   The product development and production process in a clothing factory.

way in which ready-to-wear fashion designers operate, though designer labels tend to sell in much smaller quantities and therefore work with small specialist manufacturers.)

Liaising with garment suppliers

Buyers may deal directly with representatives from any of the following, when buying merchandise, at home or overseas:

- garment manufacturers;
- retailer's overseas sourcing office;
- agents;
- indirect importers;
- wholesalers.

The buyer usually liaises with a representative from the sales department of the manufacturer and may also be in direct contact with designers or garment technologists from the company. Most retailers source some garments within their ranges from other countries, and this is one of the main opportunities for travel by the buyer. Time must be planned very carefully on business trips as companies invest a large amount of money in travel and every hour must be used to the maximum. Evenings and weekends are likely to be spent socialising with business associates or working. There is a huge difference between holidays and sourcing trips. Occasionally a buyer may be fortunate enough to take some of their holiday entitlement immediately after a business trip at a nearby location. However this is seldom the case as the buyer will have plenty of work to catch up on in the office. The timing of the trip is important – it needs to be early enough to put garments into work with enough time to develop and finalise the range afterwards. Although there are several disadvantages to buying fashion merchandise from overseas suppliers, price is usually the most significant factor in making buying decisions and can far outweigh any potential problems.

Developments in the UK clothing industry

Garment manufacturing diminished in the UK during the 1980s and 1990s, as exemplified by Marks and Spencer's severance in 1999 of a long-standing contract with the UK manufacturer, William Baird, resulting in the purchase of more goods in other countries. Coats Viyella (CV) ceased to produce merchandise for Marks and Spencer in 2000, resulting in the closure of several factories and many job losses, despite having been the retailer's largest supplier. Such a profound loss of manufacturing is likely to affect the UK clothing industry's status as the fifth largest employer in the UK. There are however hundreds of clothing factories still in business in the UK distributed throughout the country but concentrated mainly around London, the east Midlands and Manchester. The companies which are successful in this country usually compete more on service than price, offering a fast turnaround of products, a design service and/or good quality. An increasing number of companies offer a combination of UK-based and overseas production, particularly with East European countries, using a UK-based design team and making initial orders at a competitive price abroad but producing repeat orders in this country.

Wholesalers

Some buyers purchase products from wholesalers who are effectively middle men between manufacturers and retailers. The wholesaler buys quantities of garments from manufacturers which are then kept in stock, to be sold to retailers. Some manufacturers also have wholesale divisions which can provide an effective way to fill production gaps at various times of year so that there is still plenty of work for the factory at quiet periods. The wholesaler's premises take the form of a warehouse filled with bulk quantities of garments which are available for immediate delivery to retailers.

Wholesalers may also have a showroom with samples of current styles to show to buyers and, possibly, samples of garments to be produced in the future. Buying from a wholesaler is a method used mainly by small-scale retailers, particularly fashion stores with one outlet or market traders because it is pos- sible to buy small quantities of garments from stock. Some wholesalers are willing to sell as few as ten pieces of a garment, though the wholesaler may charge a little extra for such a small order. The garments cost more from a wholesaler than if the retailer ordered them directly from the manufacturer but most small-scale retailers would be unlikely to buy big enough quantities to order directly from a factory. The advantage of buying from a wholesaler is that the garments are available from stock rather than having to order months in advance, and if the retailer sells out of a style it may be possible to order more garments at short notice.

Buying fashion merchandise overseas

Price is generally the main advantage in buying fashion merchandise overseas. There are also manufacturing techniques and skills which are available only in certain countries, e.g. embroidered cotton products from India, and the prestige of buying from fashion-orientated countries such as Italy. Buying fashion merchandise overseas does have a number of disadvantages, however:

- long-distance delivery costs;
- import charges, such as duties and quotas (in some cases);
- longer delivery time;
- quality standards can be more difficult to monitor;
- time and expense incurred by buyer in travelling to overseas markets and communicating;
- buying in a different currency.

Other potential problems when buying products from overseas include:

- language barriers;
- time difference;

- unethical practices (e.g. child labour);
- political unrest and war;
- strikes (e.g. lorry drivers);
- currency fluctuations;
- variable weather conditions (e.g. flooding).

Most of the disadvantages in buying merchandise abroad can be overcome, and are usually outweighed by the price advantage. E-mail is overtaking fax, phone and letters as the prime method of international communication. When buyers are away assistants are usually left to oversee ranges in their absence, which can give them an opportunity to gain valuable experience in carrying out the buyer's role on a short-term basis. During buying trips overseas buyers are usually in regular contact with head office, but assistant buyers may find that situations arise which require a rapid response, resulting in the need for decisions to be taken during a buyer's absence.

The advantages and disadvantages of buying fashion merchandise from the home market are generally the opposite of those for buying from other countries. In theory, delivery time should be reduced when purchasing goods from the same country and it should be easier to monitor quality standards. However if goods are delivered by air freight from the Far East this can take just a few days longer than goods being transported by road in the same country. In Hong Kong a limited amount of goods is allowed to be exported to the UK which is referred to as quota. Manufacturers in Hong Kong are permitted to have a certain amount of quota, that is to export a certain quantity of garments to the UK, and a trade has developed where quota is sold on the open market. The cost of quota varies from one season to another depending on demand for it and also varies according to the product category of the merchandise. Products from the Far East may still cost less even after taking into account the additional costs of quota and sea or air freight.

In my own experience sample garments could often be received more quickly from manufacturers in Hong Kong than from the UK, despite the difference in distance. International courier services which can deliver in as short a time as two days make overseas manufacturers very competitive in terms of speed of sample development. In some cases this offers buyers more opportunity for travel, though a decline in profits for some UK retailers has reduced the amount of overseas travel involved, with manufacturers being expected to undertake travel abroad on behalf of the retailers. There is no guarantee of improved quality within the same country as the retailer and QCs are unlikely to be able to see every garment style within the range in production. Some of the potential problems mentioned above can apply to buying products in the UK, for instance unethical practices, strikes and adverse weather conditions can affect almost any country. Products are almost always more expensive to manufacture in Western than in Eastern countries, mainly due to higher labour costs. It could be considered unethical to purchase products from countries where machinists are paid low wages, yet by deciding to buy products elsewhere the buyer could deprive these workers of their only source of income. The wages of the machinists should also be considered in relation to their cost of living which is much lower in most Eastern countries than in the Western hemisphere, but buyers should make decisions about garment sourcing in the light of the moral and ethical issues involved.

Overseas sourcing offices

The role of the merchandiser in a retailer's overseas sourcing office varies substantially from the role of a head office-based merchandiser. In an overseas sourcing office merchandisers represent the retailer whilst understanding the market of the country in which they are based, both in terms of language and culture. This type of merchandiser is often a native of the country where the office is located, but many companies also employ expatriates in key roles within an overseas sourcing office. Merchandisers from the overseas sourcing office usually liaise with buyers, merchandisers and QCs from the retailer's head office on a daily basis. The advantage to the buyer is that they can communicate via just one person in that country rather than with several representatives from manufacturers. Merchandisers from the overseas office sometimes visit buyers at the company's head office to be briefed on the direction of the next season's range, thereby allowing them to consult manufacturers and prepare effectively before the buyer travels to the country on a buying trip. Overseas sourcing offices are owned by relatively large retailers as the overheads are reasonably high and can only be met by companies which buy garments in large quantities. Many large store groups have their own offices in the capitals of the world's main clothing manufacturers, such as Delhi and Hong Kong. During visits overseas buyers may have meetings with the manufacturers either at the retailer's office base or at the manufacturer's showroom (which is often based within the factory premises). The retailer's overseas merchandiser is usually present at this meeting to take notes, help with liaison (particularly language problems) and to follow up on behalf of the buyer after the meeting. Figure 7.2 shows a UK buyer visiting a manufacturer's showroom in India, accompanied by a merchandiser from the overseas sourcing office. Buyers contact overseas manufacturers regularly, either directly or through the overseas merchandise office. This is to follow up on the progress of issues such as approvals of lab dyes, strike-offs, fitting samples and fabric tests, primarily by e-mail, but also by fax and phone. Sometimes the manufacturers or the overseas sourcing office merchandisers visit the UK to discuss a range of relevant issues.

Figure 7.2 Photograph of a buyer in a garment manufacturer's showroom in India

Agents and indirect importers

Buyers can also work with agents, based either in the UK or abroad. The agents are paid by the suppliers with whom they work on a salary and/or commission basis. The advantage of working in this way is that the retailer does not need to invest in setting up an office abroad. However agents sell products from a limited number of companies, which may give the buyer less scope for initiating relationships with new suppliers. An agent effectively undertakes a sales role for the manufacturers, and is usually paid on a commission-only basis, increasing the incentive for selling a high quantity of merchandise to the buyer. Indirect importers work in a similar way to agents. They are based in the home country, developing products to sell to retailers and then organising the manufacture of the garments overseas, probably working with more than one factory. The manufacturer pays the indirect importer a percentage of the income which has been generated by this method. The indirect importer is therefore taking on the garment sourcing role from the buyer, and products sold in this way cost slightly more than if the buyer were working directly with factories abroad, to cover the indirect importer's costs.

Exchange rates

At the start of a buying season the buyer is briefed on the season's exchange rates, usually by the imports or merchandise department. As exchange rates fluctuate it is essential that buyers refer to the latest rate or their calculations (and therefore profit margins) will be incorrect. Foreign currency is purchased in advance by retailers so the rate a buyer uses is based on the rate at the time of purchase of the currency and therefore does not change daily.

Minimum and initial orders

When a buyer selects a garment style, the garment quantity is decided after discussion with the merchandiser. If the garment is being produced exclusively for a retailer this should be at least the minimum production quantity permitted by the manufacturer. It could be as few as 300 but is more often 500 or 1,000 pieces per style. If the buyer is selecting a garment from an existing range, usually with a different label from that of the retailer, the minimum quantity is much lower, possibly about ten garments. This is because the manufacturer is producing many more of the same garment, to be sold to several different stores. Manufacturers have minimum order quantities because it is not usually financially viable to produce small quantities, as the machinists do not have the opportunity to attain an economical speed of manufacture with a relatively small run. Also overheads, such as the costs of pattern cutting and grading, which are usually borne by the manufacturer, are relatively high if spread over a small number of garments. At designer level, the ready-to-wear sector of the fashion market, design development and pattern cutting take place at the designer's studio and manufacturers can make very small quantities – as little as 20 pieces – for which they charge a premium price. At this level of the market manufacture usually takes place in small factories with highly skilled machinists who may need to be more versatile in their sewing skills than in a mass-production clothing factory.

Placing repeat orders with suppliers

The buyer must make an informed decision about how many garments to order initially, perhaps choosing to be cautious by ordering the minimum amount possible. However if the product sells well and the initial estimate was over-cautious the retailer may be in danger of being out of stock of a successful line, consequently losing orders and therefore missing out on potential profits. If an initial order of a garment style sells well the buyer or merchandiser may consider purchasing a repeat order which will usually be purchased from the original garment manufacturer, though this can vary. If the initial order was bought from Hong Kong for example the delivery time for a repeat could be too long for the product to arrive in store for the current season. In this case the buyer may decide to order the product from the original supplier but have it delivered by air rather than sea, thereby speeding up the delivery schedule by weeks. Although air freight is expensive, the garment obviously appeals to the retailers' customers, and it is likely to continue to sell well. The buyer may therefore be prepared to take a lower profit margin, though this may require approval from either the senior buyer or buying manager.

If the design idea for this style belongs to the retailer the buyer may place a repeat order in the UK for a style originally made overseas, and although the production costs are likely to be more expensive, delivery time should – in theory – be quicker. However the manufacturer may need to add time to the production schedule to develop patterns and samples as the overseas supplier is unlikely to be willing to send copies of patterns to a competitor. In this example the buyer needs to draw on experience, and possibly advice from colleagues, as to which country to choose for a repeat order. The main method of assessing the need for repeat orders is to calculate the number of weeks of 'cover' available for a garment, that is, how many more weeks the garment is likely to stay in stock. Some retailers see ten weeks cover as being ideal; so from an initial order of 3,000 garments, 300 pieces will have sold in the first week. This is a simplistic example, as sales usually tend to be boosted when the product first arrives in store, only to trail off later in the season. However this is not always the case as some products may be delivered prior to a trend taking hold, or magazine coverage of a garment may generate high mid-season sales figures. The timing for repeat orders is crucial and if the manufacturer does not deliver by a specified time the product may be literally 'past its sell-by date'. Racks of garments in the January sales may not be caused solely by the buyer selecting the wrong type of product for the customer, but may also be due to repeat orders arriving too late for the season.

Departments within a garment manufacturer

The departmental structure of a garment factory varies from one company to another and is often dependent on the size of the organisation, large-scale manufacturers usually having more departments than smaller companies. Companies with fewer than 100 employees require versatile individuals who may be expected to take on dual roles, for instance production and quality control manager, or designer/pattern cutter. A clothing manufacturer is typically divided into the following departments:

- design;
- sales and marketing;
- costings;
- purchasing;
- QC;

- cutting room;
- production;
- finishing;
- warehouse.

In smaller factories some of these departments may be merged, so the design department could also be responsible for producing garment costings. Ordinarily, each section is based on the same site, although – as mentioned above – some companies have factories in different countries from the design and sales office. All of the manufacturer's departments should interact in order to complete orders successfully. It is a sign of a positive working environment in a factory when the design and sales staff liaise with QC and production during the design and sampling process.

Design department

A factory may have one designer or a design team headed by a manager. The design department is usually located in a separate room (or sometimes a separate building) from production, with storage facilities for fabric samples, patterns and reference material. Designers may be responsible for cutting patterns for their designs, or there may be a specialist pattern cutter/grader. Each designer liaises with one or more retailers. The first sample of a design is usually made to the designer's specifications by a sample machinist, based in the design room, who completes all of the sewing operations within the garment. Designers need to be aware of production constraints such as the type of sewing machines available in the factory in order to design garments which are suitable for bulk production and sample machinists can be very helpful in this respect at the design stage. Designers are involved throughout the product development stage of a garment and are often consulted during production, for example to check if the bulk fabric delivery and trims are of the correct type.

Sales and marketing

Smaller manufacturers may have one sales representative whereas a large-scale clothing supplier may have a large sales and marketing department headed by a sales or marketing director. The sales team are responsible for liaising with retailers to sell the company's products and for negotiating prices. Sales representatives need to know the potential volume of production available in the factory so that they can assess how many garments they need to sell to keep the machinists in work. Meetings with retailers are usually attended jointly by a sales representative and designer, with the sales representative concentrating on prices and order quantities while the designer discusses styling and fabrics.

Sales representatives are involved mainly during the product development phase of garments but also take an active interest in production, as they are responsible for liaising with merchandisers to ensure that the agreed deadline and delivery dates will be met.

Costings

The manufacturer may have a separate costing team, or costing may be incorporated into a design, sales or production role. Garment suppliers submit costings to retailers by estimating accurately the price of manufacturing the garment plus all of the materials and trims, and a profit margin to make the sale financially viable. Buyers frequently request cost prices within a short space of time but for the price to be accurate a garment sample must be made first and analysed by a work study engineer, so a realistic cost price cannot be given from a garment sketch. However an experienced sales representative or designer may be able to estimate the cost price from a sketch instinctively, allowing them to give a ballpark figure to the buyer.

Stages in producing a costing

(1) The design department documents relevant information such as the price of buttons and material, and estimates the average quantity of fabric required per garment. The designer has a great deal of influence on the costing through the selection of fabric, trims and design details within the garment.

(2) Once the sample garment has been made the sample machinist lists every separate process involved and hands this over to a work study engineer (sometimes called a garment technician) who estimates how long a garment will take, on average, to complete in bulk production. Because every machinist works at varying speeds the time can only ever be estimated, based on numerous time studies which the work study engineer has compiled from observing machinists on previous production runs. The average time which a machinist is expected to take to sew a garment is estimated in what are known as 'standard minutes'.

(3) The estimated standard minutes are then communicated to the costings department, where they are combined with the information from design, and a computer program is used to calculate a suggested price.

(4) The sales representative analyses the costing sheet and presents an initial price to the buyer. This price is based largely on the estimated production and material costs but is also influenced by how much the customer is expected to pay. The salesperson negotiates with the buyer until a price is

finalised which is agreeable to both parties. The final selling price from the manufacturer to the retailer is referred to as the cost price.

Purchasing

The person responsible for purchasing the fabric and components necessary to make garments is often referred to as a buyer, yet the role differs substantially from the job of the fashion buyer employed by a retailer. Large manufacturers may have a department devoted to this task and in others it may form part of the sales or production role. A buyer working for a manufacturer is essentially an administrator who completes the necessary paperwork to order specified fabrics and trims, and may become involved in negotiating the most competitive prices for these products from the suppliers.

Quality control

Factories usually employ more than one QC, depending on the size of the company, responsible for checking the standard of merchandise being produced. In a large company there may be a QC manager responsible for co-ordinating the QC team and setting standards of garment make-up. The QC manager liaises with retailers' QC teams when they visit factories for in-work checks. Some manufacturers employ garment technologists in a similar role.

Cutting room

Although most garment factories have their own cutting rooms in which fabric is laid out and cut for bulk orders, some companies specialise only in cutting garments, used either by small factories which concentrate purely on making garments, or by larger factories which need extra cutting capacity at busy periods. When the grades for a garment have been approved the patterns are arranged in what is known as a 'lay plan' to achieve the minimum of fabric wastage by a 'marker maker' (who may be based in the cutting room) either manually or by computer. For bulk production fabric is laid out in several piles by specialist spreading machines before cutting, and the lay plan is placed on top. Most factories use a straightknife, powered by an electric motor, which a cutter uses to cut through many layers of fabric at once guided by the lay plan. Laser cutting, water jet cutting and ultrasonic cutting are new developments which may eventually supersede the straightknife. Cut work is labelled and bundled and sent for garment production.

Garment production

A production manager is responsible for planning and implementing garment production. Factories are usually organised in production lines where machinists are seated in rows and work is delivered to them in bundles by supervisors. (See Figure 7.3). The basic types of sewing machine used in the industry are lockstitchers and overlockers. The lockstitch machine has a basic stitch similar to that of a domestic machine, and is used for joining seams, topstitching, and many other garment manufacturing techniques. An overlocker finishes the raw edges of seams and hems so that they do not fray.

Figure 7.3 A clothing factory production line

There are also numerous types of specialist sewing machine including seam-cover machines and flatseamers which are suitable for making garments in stretch fabrics. The type of sewing machines used by a factory can vary according to the type of garments produced. Garment factories tend to specialise in either woven or knitted fabrics, and it is essential that the buyer is aware of a manufacturer's specialisation in fabric and garment type when placing a style in production. Make-up of garments is split into separate operations so that some machinists specialise in making up certain elements of a garment, such as collars, or certain types of machining such as overlocking the seams together. Supervisors are experienced machinists responsible for organising a production line. A more traditional method of factory organisation is for an individual machinist or a small team, to 'make through' garments from start to finish. A team of pressers iron the finished garments and some garments may be sent through a steam tunnel. Completed garments are checked during and after production by QCs, and faulty garments are returned to the machinists who produced them, to be corrected. Defective garments which cannot be corrected, or which have fabric faults, are referred to as seconds and are not submitted to the retailer.

Warehousing and delivery

Finished garments are bagged in transparent plastic garment covers to keep them clean, then stored in the factory's warehouse either in boxes or on hangers. A final garment inspection by the factory's or retailer's QC's may take place in the warehouse. The garments are then delivered to the retailer's warehouse where there may be a final QC inspection before distribution of the products to stores.

Summary

Buyers make decisions on garment sourcing based mainly on the price, quality and service of the manufacturer. High street retailers usually develop garment ideas in conjunction with manufacturers, liaising mostly with designers and sales representatives. Most garments sold in the UK are imported, though clothing production still forms a significant part of the country's economy. Many garment suppliers have a UK-based design and sales team, but use overseas production. The product development and production processes run simultaneously with the retailer's buying cycle.

Chapter 8
Buying for Retail Fashion Multiples

Retail fashion multiples (also known as fashion chainstores) have numerous outlets and although they vary in terms of target market, buying systems and departmental structure, the main principles of fashion buying for multiples remain broadly the same. Within this book the fashion multiple is defined as a fashion retailer with more than twenty stores, although most have over 100 branches. Fashion multiples dominate the clothing market in the UK and this sector contains the highest proportion of fashion buying jobs in this country. Compared to the UK multiples tend to be less predominant in other European countries where there is more of an emphasis on independent fashion retailers selling branded merchandise.

Major UK store groups

Most fashion multiples are subsidiaries of a parent company which often has a different name from its high street stores. The domination of the UK fashion market by store groups peaked during the 1980s and 1990s, with four major parent companies owning the majority of specialist fashion stores during that era. These included the Burton Group, Next, Sears and Storehouse. By 2000, UK store groups had consolidated, leaving only two of these companies with a significant portfolio of stores. The Burton Group demerged from department store Debenhams during the 1990s, changing its name to the Arcadia Group, and leaving Debenhams as a plc in its own right. Arcadia retained all of the fashion chains owned by the Burton Group (Top Shop, Top Man, Burton, Dorothy Perkins and Evans) and acquired Sears' womenswear chains: (Miss Selfridge, Richards, Wallis and Warehouse) in 1998. Arcadia also diversified into mail order and e-retailing by buying Racing Green and Hawkshead mail order businesses, and offering free internet access through its transactional website, zoom.com. Next successfully survived the 1990s with its men's, women's and children's fashion stores intact, as well as its interiors range and mail order catalogue. Storehouse now owns only Mothercare stores, having sold Habitat to Ikea and Bhs to Philip Green. The Sears group (not to be confused with its American namesake) disbanded during the 1990s and its stores were sold to several different companies, including the purchase of Dolcis footwear stores by the UK fashion chain, Alexon, and a management buyout at Adams Childrenswear. The demise of Sears changed the footwear retail sector in the UK as shoes were traditionally sold mainly in specialist stores. The majority of fashion retailers now sell their own footwear to coordinate directly with their clothing ranges.

Finding information on store groups

Corporate ownership of fashion stores in the UK is subject to frequent change and it is essential for those who want to remain aware of the current structure of companies in the high street to read the trade press and broadsheet financial pages, or to visit fashion retailers' websites for the latest information. Some stores have been subject to numerous retail takeovers and demergers; Richards once belonged to Storehouse before being sold to Sears, and is now a casualty of the ever-changing retail sector, having been completely closed down in 2000. Store groups' annual reports detail the company structure and list subsidiaries. If a store group is a public limited company (plc) annual reports are automatically available to members of the general public by contacting the head office, and many are available on the companies' websites. Annual reports provide financial information about the parent company, including annual turnover and profit, and often contain written and visual information about the subsidiaries. Annual reports are not published separately for individual fashion retail chains within a store group and it is therefore important when researching into a store which is a subsidiary to be aware of the parent company. This can be discovered simply by asking sales staff in the store or by looking at company literature such as a storecard application form.

In addition to specialist fashion chains several other retailers are major players in the UK led by Marks and Spencer (a variety chain) which currently has a bigger percentage of the UK clothing market than any other retailer (Mintel, 1999). Marks and Spencer suffered from a poor media profile in the late 1990s, due to falling profits and a reduction in UK garment production, yet at the same time it remained profitable in a difficult economic climate in the retail sector, while other fashion retailers, notably including Arcadia, were struggling to break even. Marks and Spencer sells interiors products and groceries in addition to clothing and has long held a reputation for producing quality merchandise.

Categories of fashion multiples

Fashion multiples can be classified into several categories, depending on the range of merchandise which is offered.

Specialist fashion multiples

As its name suggests, the specialist fashion multiple concentrates on selling fashion merchandise. Stores within this category can be classified within the following price brackets:

Lower mass market

- Matalan
- New Look
- Bay Trading
- Hennes
- Mark One

Middle mass market

- River Island
- Jeffrey Rogers
- Zara
- Arcadia group (Top Shop, Top Man, Burton, Dorothy Perkins, Principles, Warehouse, Wallis, Evans)
- Mothercare
- Adams
- Next
- Morgan
- Kookai
- Oasis
- Gap

Upper mass market

- French Connection
- Monsoon
- Jigsaw
- Hobbs
- Episode
- Karen Millen

This list is not exhaustive but gives an indication of stores and their direct competitors within particular price ranges. Stores at the lower end of the mass market have reportedly been the most successful fashion multiples during the late 1990s, with consumers focusing on value for money. Middle mass market retailers did not perform as well as value retailers during this period, with the possible exception of Next. River Island is a rare example of a private fashion multiple and unlike its plc competitors has no legal requirement to publish its accounts to the public. The middle mass market has the highest concentration of fashion multiples in the UK making it an overcrowded sector, though it is aimed at the largest segment of fashion consumers. Although Karen Millen's price range is substantially higher than Monsoon's both have been classified in the upper mass market, which includes relatively few fashion multiples in this country. There is a current trend towards diversification in specialist fashion multiples by selling fashion-orientated products in addition to clothing, so Oasis sells jewellery, sunglasses, luggage and footwear, and New Look launched a range of decorative household items in 2000. Accordingly, buyers with experience in working with fashion products other than clothing are increasingly in demand.

Franchises

Specialist fashion multiples occasionally operate on a franchise basis, where the store is run by a franchisee, who purchases all of the products from the franchisor (the originator of the store's concept and image). The franchise contract obliges the franchisee to pay an initial start-up fee and subsequent royalties to the franchisor. This may seem a relatively expensive method of setting up a retail business, yet it could be argued that the franchise has a good chance of success from trading under an established brand name, with the overheads of range planning, product development and promotion being borne by the franchisor. Franchising is rare within the fashion market, the most well-known example being the Italian company Benetton. The advantage to the franchisor is that the brand can expand with the minimum of investment in new stores, as well as the benefit of regular income from franchisees.

Variety chains

Variety chains are stores which sell a variety of fashion and household products, primarily under the retailer's own label. The most famous UK-based variety chain is Marks and Spencer. Its main competitors are Bhs (originally called British Home Stores) which sells products at a similar price level, and Littlewoods, which is in a cheaper price bracket. Littlewoods remains a private family-owned variety chain selling men's, women's and children's clothing and footwear as well as household products. Littlewoods is also well-known for its mail order catalogues and Index catalogue stores. Woolworths is a variety chain with a unique mix of products, and although it stocks mainly household items it offers a significant amount of clothing, most notably its Ladybird range of childrenswear. Boots could also be classified within this category; though it is known largely for toiletries, it also offers childrenswear, with an emphasis on babywear.

Department stores

A department store is a retail outlet that sells numerous types of product, concentrating mainly on clothing and household goods. Most of the products are from a variety of brands but the department store usually also sells merchandise under its own brand. Department stores thrived as fashion retailers during the first half of the twentieth century, but declined in popularity from the 1970s with the rise of the specialist fashion multiples. There are still several major department store groups in the UK, including Debenhams, Fenwick, House of Fraser and John Lewis. These stores are renowned for their selections of fashion merchandise which often comprise a variety of price ranges, but they tend to concentrate mainly on the mass market to middle market price bracket. During the late 1990s, some UK department stores opened new branches, including a new Harvey Nichols outlet in Leeds, and a branch of Selfridges in Manchester. (Fashion-orientated department stores in major cities are listed in Chapter 4, Table 4.1.)

Most buyers for department stores select products from branded ranges (see Chapter 11). Department stores also employ buyers to develop in-house ranges which may be sold under the store's own name or under another label, for example House of Fraser's Linea and Platinum ranges. Some department stores such as Debenhams offer several of their own ranges as their stores cater for a wide range of customer types. Department stores have different buying teams for separate ranges, giving the impression of offering several different stores under one roof.

Concessions

Many department stores operate concessions where space within the store is leased to another retailer, so House of Fraser has Morgan and Giant concessions within some of its outlets. This part of the store is likely to have its own separate retail image and the sales staff are employed by the company running the concession. Traditionally the concession method has been used by middle market womenswear brands aimed at a conservative, mature market, some of which also operate stand-alone stores, including Jaeger, Alexon, Planet and Jacques Vert.

Supermarkets

Supermarkets are becoming increasingly important in the UK fashion market. The major competitors in the supermarket sector are Tesco, Asda and Sainsbury's Savacentre. The George range from Asda (incorporating men's, women's and children's clothing and footwear) currently has the most significant share of the clothing market amongst UK supermarkets (Mintel, 1999). Asda was bought by the American value retailer, Wal-Mart, in 2000, opening up the possibility of the George range being sold in the USA. In 2001, Sainsbury's launched a new range of clothing designed by Jeff Banks. Supermarkets benefit from having a large number of frequent customers who can be tempted to make impulse purchases of clothes whilst buying the weekly shopping, and therefore have a much higher 'footfall' of customers than most stores which sell fashion merchandise. Supermarkets' profit margins tend to be lower than other mass market retailers due to high sales volume, and they can therefore offer better value in their clothing ranges than high street competitors. The buying power of Tesco has allowed the company to buy in products from the so-called 'grey market', which involves buying designer branded goods from middle-men rather than from the direct source, and selling it on to the public at much reduced prices. Designer brands do not support this practice as it appears to cheapen the appeal of their products and are usually unwilling to sell directly to supermarkets.

Outlet stores

The American-style 'outlet village' concept arrived in the UK in the 1990s. Outlet villages are generally located in out-of-town sites in the form of purpose-built shopping centres selling a wide range of discounted designer-level, middle market and mass market products. Prices are low because most of the merchandise on sale is from previous seasons, enabling designer-level companies to retain an upmarket appearance in their standard stores, which are usually located in London, well away from the outlet village. Bicester shopping village in Oxfordshire includes stores as diverse as Jeffrey Rogers and Christian Lacroix.

International fashion multiples

Certain fashion multiples from the USA and Europe have expanded worldwide and several have made an impact on the UK market, competing directly with home-grown fashion chains. Well-known international fashion multiples include:

- Mango, Zara (Spain)
- Benetton (Italy)

- Kookai, Morgan (France)
- Gap, Banana Republic, Victoria's Secret (USA)
- Hennes & Mauritz (H&M), (Sweden)

Many UK fashion multiples also have overseas branches, including Marks and Spencer, Bhs, Top Shop and Evans.

Sales markdowns

During January and July most fashion stores hold their major sales in order to clear stocks ready for the new season's merchandise. In recent years certain retailers have begun to discount merchandise in the run-up to Christmas, traditionally the most successful selling period, reflecting the fact that some retailers face increasing competition from the lower mass market level. Additionally some stores hold mid-season sales, usually in April and October, to dispose of slow-selling lines while they are still relevant to current fashion trends and appropriate for the seasonal weather. If this merchandise were held back until the end-of-season sale the retailer would probably have to sell it at a lower price to persuade customers to purchase a style which had become out of date. The mid-season sale therefore allows garments to be sold off with the minimum reduction and the turnover from it becomes available to buy new products rather than being tied up in redundant stock. Next takes the approach of reorganising the store format for a short time during sale periods to present reduced merchandise on long rails while the new season's full-price range is displayed more attractively in a separate section of the store. Other retailers such as Miss Selfridge have a limited amount of stock on sale at most times during the year but tend to keep this in a more discreet location at the back of the store or on an upper floor level.

Product assortment

Retailers can offer a 'narrow and deep' or 'broad and shallow' product assortment. A narrow and deep buying policy refers to buying a relatively small number of styles in high volume. This minimises the amount of development of different products and is more efficient to manufacture in bulk. As this method is usually more cost-effective it can lead to higher profits for the companies involved and/or lower prices for the store's customers. However the production of a large quantity of the same garment results in a lack of exclusivity, which is very important to certain sectors of the fashion market. Retailers with a narrow and deep product assortment include UK chain stores focusing on classic merhandise, such as Marks and Spencer and Bhs who buy most garments in quantities of tens of thousands. In the late 1990s both of these retailers suffered from much-publicised lower profits and suspected takeover bids, resulting in a review of their buying strategies. Whilst garment manufacturers view the opportunity to make products in high quanitities as very attractive reliance on a single major retailer for business can be dangerous, as evidenced by the closure of William Baird and Coats Viyella's dedicated Marks and Spencer divisions.

Buying to a 'broad and shallow' policy means offering a wide selection of garment styles in limited numbers per style. This involves a great deal of development from the fashion buyer and the company's suppliers, with less efficiency and therefore less cost-effectiveness in manufacturing. The products will possibly cost more or be of a slightly lower quality standard than if they were made in larger quantities, but the customer is offered a wider choice of garments within the store. A broad and shallow policy is suitable for the younger, more design-led high street retailers such as Oasis and Top Shop, which usually buy products in quantities of a few thousand per style. As the buyer is allowed to order a wider selection of products per season, this allows the range to be constantly updated in response to changing trends. Some retailers achieve a balance by adopting a buying policy somewhere between the two methods described above. A store such as Gap could be considered to work to a narrow and deep policy, but gives the customer a wide product choice by offering a wide range of colourways per product, particularly in womenswear.

Retail fashion multiples give their stores different classifications, dependent upon the size and location of the store and therefore the variety of products offered, for instance 'grade A' for the largest stores through to 'grade C' for the smallest branches. Smaller stores inevitably receive a narrower range of merchandise, with more of an emphasis on classic styles and a limited number of the more fashionable items.

The seconds market

All clothing manufacturers need to dispose of seconds, which are garments of substandard quality (see Chapter 7). Many seconds are caused by poor sewing quality and others may be due to fabric faults which were not identified before garment manufacture. Manufacturers' and retailers' QC departments aim to eradicate most quality problems before garments are delivered to stores, leaving manufacturers with a certain amount of stock considered unacceptable to the original retailer and needing to be sold elsewhere to recoup some of the costs. Most retailers ask for their labels to be cut out of the garments so that they do not compete directly with the same products in their high street stores, but discerning customers find the remains of the label easily identifiable. Some retailers have agreements with their manufacturers to retain seconds for a certain period, so that they will not be sold at the same time as the perfect merchandise.

Factory shops

Some clothing manufacturers have their own factory shops which can utilise space within the building thereby generating lower overheads than renting a store in a shopping centre. Prices are therefore particularly low, often around 50 per cent of high street prices, to account for the lower quality of the merchandise and the relatively low costs of running the shops. Premises are usually very basic which most customers expect at such low prices. Factory shops cannot be visually merchandised in cohesive garment ranges in the same way as in ordinary retail stores as they cannot anticipate in detail the styles and quantities which will come into stock. Despite such shops usually being out-of-town, customers often hear of them by word-of-mouth and are willing to travel some way for the satisfaction of finding a bargain. The manufacturer's own employees, who are usually given the incentive of staff discount, also provide a ready market for the factory shop.

Certain large manufacturing groups such as Courtaulds have their own chains of factory shops offering the same range of merchandise in stores located at their manufacturing plants. Because such large manufacturers make a wide variety of garment types, they can offer complete outfits in their stores. Sometimes smaller garment manufacturers with a few stores buy seconds directly from other manufacturers to expand the range of products on offer to the customer. Manufacturers also sometimes make garment ranges specifically to be sold in their factory shops, often using leftover fabric from previous seasons or fabric bought at a discount from fabric merchants, to keep the factory in work during slack periods. In the UK many factory shops are based around the North and Midlands where most of the country's garment manufacture is concentrated. Some factory shops employ buyers who may combine the role with managing the shop, though there is obviously far less product development involved, if any, compared with buying for a high street retailer. Factory shops usually have no advertising to keep their overheads low but books are published with lists of their locations. The factory shop system operates in many different countries, including Hong Kong. Some seconds retailers do not own factories but run their own stores, buying merchandise from garment manufacturers and/or wholesalers and selling it for slightly more than in factory shops but substantially less than most high street retailers.

Retail sales performance

As explained in Chapter 3 the performance of a range is often assessed by comparing current sales figures to those in the same period during the previous year, usually in terms of the amount of financial turnover. Retailers can also calculate sales per square metre of floor space within stores. This takes into account the amount of available selling space, which may have increased due to store openings or extensions, enabling like-for-like comparisons to be made with the previous year. Sales per square metre can be calculated by the following method:

$$\frac{\text{Total sales within a chosen period}}{\text{Number of square metres in which products are sold}} = \text{Sales per square metre}$$

Calculating sales per square metre is useful for fashion multiples when assessing the profitability of merchandise where separate ranges are sold either within a store or within different stores. Such figures would enable a department store selling several brands to assess which made the most successful use of the space available, and to replace those which were not performing well with new ranges or to extend more successful brands into this space.

Visual merchandising and point-of-sale

The way in which products are displayed in stores can have a marked effect on the performance of a garment range. This is the responsibility of the visual merchandiser (VM), and the buyer is rarely involved in this process despite the potential impact upon sales. VMs organise the display of products on the shopfloor and in windows. Some retailers have senior VMs who produce a corporate look for all of the retailer's stores, and this is communicated to VMs to be implemented within all of the branches so that a consistent image is maintained. A store's window display is one of the key elements in enticing customers into the store. This valuable space is usually reserved for the season's key fashion items and is updated regularly. Once customers are in the store it is acknowledged that the majority of them are likely to purchase more basic products than those in the window, but the display serves its purpose by attracting the customer inside.

'Point-of-sale' promotional material is that which is displayed and distributed within stores. This includes photographs of garments which have been featured in magazines and brochures and displays promoting particular brands. Point-of-sale promotional techniques provide the retailer with the final opportunity to persuade the customer to make a purchase, at the last stage in the decision-making process. Some point-of-sale methods continue to influence the customer after leaving the store, such as leaflets which often promote store-cards which can encourage the customer's loyalty to the store, and brochures featuring the current range may be put into the carrier bag with a purchased item to persuade the customer to make a return visit.

Summary

Retail fashion multiples fit into the lower, middle and upper price brackets within the mass market and can be classified in several categories:

- specialist fashion multiples;
- variety chains;
- department stores;
- supermarkets;
- outlet stores.

Retailers buy product assortments which are either narrow and deep or broad and shallow. Sales markdowns at certain times of year allow stores to remove products with poor sales figures to be replaced by new stock. Visual merchandising and point-of-sale techniques are used by retailers to maximise sales.

Case studies in buying for retail fashion multiples

1. Oasis

Beth has been buying manager of knitwear, jerseywear and swimwear at Oasis Stores plc since 1999. Beth studied on an art foundation course at Bristol Polytechnic before taking a degree in textile design at Leicester Polytechnic, where she specialised in knitted and woven fabrics. She started her first job as a trainee knitwear buyer for Next plc in 1985. She progressed to working as a junior buyer and then a buyer for knitwear and jerseywear in the womenswear department of Next. In 1989 Beth joined the newly formed George Davies Partnership as a buyer for knitwear and jerseywear, working on the 'George for Asda' range. In 1995 she became a buyer at Oasis for woven garments from India as well as jerseywear. Beth was promoted in 1996 to senior buyer for jerseywear, which included the initial development of the swimwear range. The area for which Beth is now responsible covers almost 50 per cent of the garments sold by Oasis.

Roles and responsibilities

The buying team is headed by a buying director who is responsible for three buying managers for different product types, with a team of buyers, assistant buyers (ABs) and clerks (see Figure 8.1).

Figure 8.1   The personnel structure of the Oasis buying department.

The clerks, who often start as placement students for six months to a year, can progress to assistant buyer level. The buying team works regularly with three key departments: merchandise, design and QC. Beth sits in a team with the other buying managers and buyers alongside the buying director so that they can constantly communicate about the ranges. The workspace has been organised with satellites, so that Beth's knitwear and jerseywear ABs and clerks sit behind her at a separate group of desks. QC and merchandise sit further down the office. Beth also has some contact with the marketing department, supplying them with garments for photo shoots and indications of products that she expects to sell well. She views working closely with her colleagues as one of the positive aspects of her job:

> *I enjoy working in a team. I really enjoy developing the product and working with people internally as well as externally to get the product right. I really enjoy the fact that every day is different – there's a structure that we have to work to, but there are constantly-changing priorities so you cannot possibly get bored. You have to constantly adjust your day as things come up, which is quite frequently.*

Beth's primary responsibilities are to buy the knitwear and swimwear ranges and to manage the buying of jerseywear:

> *I don't actually buy jerseywear myself; I have a buyer working with me who does this, with two ABs and one clerk. I don't really get involved in the range, I have more of a support role for her and her team. It could be advice on suppliers or ranging – just keeping an eye on the department, really. I buy the knitwear, despite being a buying manager, which is a bit unusual, because I specifically wanted to keep in touch with the product, and I work with an AB and a clerk to do that range. I actually buy swimwear as well, with the help of an AB. My job is split quite equally between buying and managing. My major task is getting the right garment developed within the time. You have to negotiate and fit the garment and buy it in the right colours and quantities, but you also have to source the right suppliers and build up supplier relations. Without the right suppliers you can't do your job properly at all.*

The buying cycle

The buying cycle at Oasis starts with an initial concept meeting which can cover up to the first four months of a season. This is followed by a bi-monthly package presentation (BPP) where the designers present a clear idea of the shapes and key colours for the season. The design team show the garments in 'modules', the term used by Oasis for grouping clothes as to their end use, such as casual, going out, work wear or occasion wear, to ensure that customers are not receiving a 'mixed message'. Beth describes how the BPP meetings operate:

> There's an open discussion between buying and design. Once we've been through any issues we've got, we go away and work with our individual designers on the range to make them fit into those particular modules for a particular month. So, from that, we'll send out specs and sketches to the range suppliers we work with. Nearly all of the designs are done in-house – it's quite rare for us to use designs from suppliers.

After the BPP meeting, buyers review the samples submitted by manufacturers, based on the designers' sketches. The buyers aim to have 'reasonably correct garment samples' prior to selecting the range. The next stage is a 'prep meeting', in preparation for pre-selection, where the buying and design teams review the modules and check whether they're working, in terms of styling and colour, reformulating garments which are not considered to be right, and re-drawing them in time for pre-selection the following week. Beth explains the pre-selection and final selection process:

> We do pre-selection as a whole team, not by product, where we see all of the product that will be in store for any particular month and module, so we can see the full offer for the customer. Then we identify at pre-selection any areas that need to be booked, maybe Hong Kong or India, and get them signed off to make sure that the buying director is happy with them, or we'll rework them if needed. We normally have a six- or seven-week gap from then until final selection, which is about four months before the products go into stores. We follow the same process at final selection, where we do shorter lead time product and we go through a preparation process for final selection, to review the new samples that have come in, so products from the UK and Europe will be shown at this meeting. All of the designers and buyers are involved in final selection, as well as the directors of buying and design and the merchandise controller: about 15 people.

The Oasis buying team's next major meeting is range review, about 12 weeks before the products go into store, with correct samples in correct colours. This is the team's last chance to check the range before it goes into production, when final adjustments to garments can be made. A small proportion of the buying budget (open-to-buy) is retained for any last-minute additions to the range at this stage. Beth and her team can be working on up to three seasons simultaneously, each at different stages of the buying cycle. During April, for example, the team finalise 'high summer' and 'transitional autumn' for the current year, whilst developing the October and Christmas ranges and viewing concept presentations for the following spring. Oasis stores receive new stock every week but the buyers aim to work on two-monthly selection periods as they find this more manageable. Towards the end of the selling season buyers are judged on the number of markdowns within the range.

Supplier liaison

Beth's job involves travelling either on inspirational trips or on visits to garment manufacturers:

> *I travel to Florence, for supplier visits and to Pitti Filati, New York, Hong Kong, and also inspiration trips for swimwear to Saint Tropez. Some buyers do Miami or Los Angeles for inspirational visits. We sometimes go to Milan, and some go to Première Vision in Paris. Ten years ago, I would have said that travel was one of the best things about the job. Travel is one of the things that I have to do to get the job done and I enjoy it, but I've done it for so many years now that it's not the element that I love most. The first two or three years is fantastic, but after 15 years it's not.*

Beth deals mainly with manufacturers in the Far East, Italy and the UK, as these are the main sources of garments for her product area. She finds that Hong Kong offers 'no limitations' with a diverse range of techniques for knitted garments, including a variety of gauges, embellishments, fastenings and crochet. Oasis has its own sourcing office in Hong Kong, which has helped Beth to work more effectively with suppliers from the Far East:

> *I'm buying the majority of knitwear from Hong Kong and China. That's mainly because of what they can produce, and also because the office out there has made it easier for us. I've managed to reduce the lead times from there, which is usually a huge hindrance for buyers. They get better prices generally, but they have no flexibility and create high risk. As a result of working very closely with two or three key suppliers I've managed to get lead times right down, so I'm finding now that Hong Kong is very nearly as flexible as the UK and Europe.*

Beth sources knitwear from Italy mainly for the manufacturing quality of their products, on cut-and-sew, fully-fashioned or shaped knitwear. She describes the Italians as offering 'more interesting yarns' than the Far East and having a 'fashion edge'. Beth sources a small proportion of her range from the UK though ideally she would like to buy more:

> *I think they're finding business very hard, but I don't think the UK has invested in time in the right facilities for make-up, the right machinery and yarn development, and they haven't moved on fast enough, but we do try to maintain some business in the UK. I hope things will change, but I find it difficult to buy from here, because it's very difficult to get the product. The*

UK is comparable to the Far East on price, as quota prices are currently high in the Far East. Quota is very expensive at the moment and it's been increasing in price for the last year-and-a-half. I have been in the business so long that I have been through three or four quota cycles where the price goes through the roof every four or five years, but it's beginning to decline. There was talk about getting rid of quota, but I've heard nothing further on it.

Beth's ideal garment supplier would have a design facility which could interpret designs in the right 'Oasis handwriting'. Even though the designers produce detailed spec. sheets suppliers can sometimes make garments which do not look the same as the buyer expected:

Ideally we'd like a supplier that could interpret our ideas in the right way, or a supplier that we could just talk to about something that we like the idea of on the catwalks, and they could go away and interpret it in the right way for an Oasis store. That is hard to find.

When considering working with new suppliers Beth looks for facilities or knitwear gauges, such as fine gauge, shaping or linking, to fill in gaps within the existing supply structure. To work with Oasis, manufacturers need to sell garments within a certain price and quality band. Beth frequently receives letters and telephone calls from potential new suppliers so she sends them a standard form to complete to explain how long they've been in business, their gauges, whom they supply and their facilities. She also assesses the suppliers' speed and flexibility for making sample garments, and their production time:

The shorter the time that we can turn sampling and production around, the more reactive we can be. Sometimes suppliers approach buyers directly, and once we see a supplier that we think is potentially good, we'll ask them to do some cross-costings or sampling so that we can do a like-for-like comparison. We then get our QC involved and they would do a factory check.

Customers

Beth considers the most difficult aspect of her job to be judging what the customer will want to buy, well ahead of the selling season. She thinks that this is easier for buyers in what she describes as 'middle market mainstream retailers', who could say: 'Yes, the customer wants a turtle-neck, she had one last season, and she'll probably want a similar one with two new fashion colours'. However at Oasis the customer may want a product desperately for two or three weeks, then no longer want it after a few weeks or a few months. Beth considers judging the life cycle of the product to be one of the buyer's hardest tasks. To help with this task there are several ways in which the buying team receives feedback from customers:

On a Monday morning after the sales meeting, we have a meeting with feedback from the retail team for the previous week, including strengths, weaknesses, opportunities and threats. They'll talk about what competitors have done, what's out there in the high street. They give us feedback on people's windows, how we compare to them and things that they love or things that aren't quite right, like fit issues or colour issues. We also have a meeting where we review our own product areas, saying what we've done right and wrong, so that we learn for the next season. We have all the information typed with best-sellers and photographs, then we do an action plan to work to for the following season. Buyers also do store visits twice a season where they work in the fitting rooms, and see what customers are trying on and speak to staff. We run around and get things from the stock room, and the customers have no idea who we are.

Skills and training

Oasis offers several training courses for buyers including team-building and written skills. Numeracy and computer skills are necessary for buyers at Oasis but are not the main skills required for the job, according to Beth:

The amount of numeracy you need depends on which company you go to. It's not my strength, to be honest. I do enough of that to make it work for the job, but it's not my driving passion for the job at all. I've managed to work in companies that are very product-led, so it's fine, but I suppose that's different in companies where the job is a little less creative, so you need to pick the retailer that's right for you. We use computers for e-mailing, internally and to suppliers. Buying and design probably use computers the least.

The buyers at Oasis calculate the profitability of the range from budgets and targets. They assess the 'final intake margin' from the finalised production garment, as it can be eroded by various factors, making it differ from the original margin. The buyers have a set target margin for their ranges, which they aim to maintain.

Recruitment

For level one assistant buyers or clerks Oasis recruits either from colleges or via an agency. Some applicants do not have fashion-related degrees but have decided that they want to go into retail. For senior ABs, who need prior experience the human resources department refers to application letters which are kept on file or approach an agency. Applicants go through an initial interview followed by a second interview with a presentation on a product area or project for Oasis. They may then be called in for a third interview, particularly for a senior position. Of Oasis's six buyers and buying managers, only two currently have a fashion degree. Beth offers the following advice for anyone wishing to pursue a career in buying:

> *The others have either worked their way up through the business, or they've done marketing, so it means you don't need to have a fashion degree. We look for people with drive, who can work well with a team, have good communication skills and obviously a good eye for fashion. Focus on what you want to do before you leave college, as early as you can in your final year – don't leave it until afterwards. If you can, do a sandwich course. I didn't do it, but it counts for a lot with retailers when they employ people, because they have someone on board that they know and they can take on when they leave college. If you think you want to do buying, don't take anything else, don't get side-tracked. If people really want to do buying, they've got to keep approaching people. If you're right, you'll get there in the end.*

Future developments

Oasis has recently developed a mail order catalogue which could be a potential area for growth. They may also offer internet shopping in the future, although their website is currently used only for promotional purposes. Beth is keeping a watchful eye on new competitors entering the UK market, such as Zara and Mango, as well as Oasis's existing competitors. The company's closest competitor is considered to be Warehouse, with many customers aspiring to shop at stores in a higher price bracket such as Karen Millen and French Connection. Beth also expects River Island and Top Shop customers to aspire to shopping at Oasis.

2. George at Asda

Joanna is an assistant buyer in the ladieswear department at the George Davies Partnership (GDP), the company which develops the 'George' range for Asda plc. After studying 'A' levels (Fashion and Textile Design; Textile Art and Business Studies) she progressed directly into the second year of a BTEC National Diploma at Basingstoke College of Technology, then completed a BA(Hons) Fashion Design degree at De Montfort University. Joanna was employed as an assistant buyer at GDP in 1999 and, after a year in the job, was given responsibility for her own product area.

Roles and responsibilities

Joanna's area of responsibility covers classic woven garments, comprising mainly tailoring, soft separates and comfortable separates. In addition, the ladieswear buying team consists of a buyer for wovens (working with an assistant buyer), a knitwear buyer and a jerseywear buyer. Joanna describes her product area and potential customer:

> *The classic garments are for the mother with a couple of kids, who goes shopping and sees a couple of jumpers she likes and a suit that isn't expensive, and she can wear the trousers in the evening and wear the suit to work. There are also some garments which are quite fashionable, like dresses with very thin straps or a keyhole opening or an empire-cut. There used to be a bigger divide between fashion and classic, but there isn't so much now.*

Head of design
↑
Designer
↑
Buyer
↑
Junior buyer
↑
Assistant clerk

Figure 8.2   Personnel structure of the George buying department.

Until recently the personnel structure included senior buyers, who have now been transferred to the design centre at GDP. The purpose of the design centre is to design packages with sketches and specs well in advance of the season, including details such as buttons and thread colours, which are later handed over to the buying team. The garments are fitted by the designers, then handed over to the buyers, who pass them on to QC, before grades are made. The designers approve buttons and lab dips. Joanna's role within the buying department mainly includes negotiating prices and deliveries with suppliers, as well as administrative work. She explains the importance of working closely with garment suppliers:

> *We make sure that suppliers are on an even keel in production, that there aren't a couple of periods in the year when they're lacking business, especially if something like 80 per cent of their production is for George. We make sure that they get an even balance in production, so when we select new ranges, in particular when we do a preview range for the mail order catalogue, we don't give ten styles to one supplier and only one style to another. We ensure that they don't have a gap in their production. You have an idea of which garments to put with a certain supplier, because of their 'signature' but you have to make sure that by putting new ranges with them, that it's not going to affect anything else they've got to do in a big quantity.*

Setting retail prices is a team decision between buying, merchandise and design. The George range has certain set price points, for example a standard leg trouser would retail at £19.99, but with a more luxurious fabric or extra components this could increase to £22.99.

It is the merchandiser's role at GDP to make sure that a garment has been agreed to be made by a supplier in a quantity that can be produced within a given time. The buyers liaise with merchandisers to make sure that suppliers honour their delivery dates and keep to their production schedules. Merchandisers analyse sales and if a repeat order is needed because of the success of a garment they liaise with the suppliers to ensure that they can produce a repeat in time to make additional sales. Joanna also works very closely with the PR department, who often request samples of garments for photo shoots, an area of the job which she particularly enjoys:

> *I love to do that because that means that my garments will go out for the public to see, and I want that. We've had two garments in* Vogue *recently. We have incentive days at George every three months, when the colleagues from the stores with the best sales profits from all of the different regions come down to George Clothing. We put on dinner for them and a fashion show and we show them future ranges. I help PR to get organised for that.*

Joanna also liaises frequently with the print coordination team, which organises swing tickets and hangers, etc. As well as seeing garments from design through to production Joanna is also responsible for informing suppliers which hangers to order, so much of her time is spent raising contracts for this purpose on a computer database, in conjunction with merchandisers. The buyer's role is also to inform the supplier which swing ticket must be put on the garment, and whether or not any additional labelling would be needed, for instance for a delicate fabric. Swing tickets may also be required for garments that lack hanger appeal, such as a beaded tie wrap which was labelled with a photograph from the preview catalogue to demonstrate how it should be worn.

The buying cycle

The buying cycle at GDP commences with the design team's inspirational trips. Two days after their return the designers hold a meeting with the buying team to give them feedback on current trends at contemporary and designer level, as well as on the high street. Approximately two weeks later the designers show the buyers the initial concepts, colours and cloths for the season. The design packages are sent to suppliers who return sample garments to the designers. At the handover meeting the design team gives the initial concepts, colours and ranges to the buyers for costs to be negotiated and the designers then continue to work on the fit of the buying samples. Three days of fitting sessions are held per week, split into jersey, knits and wovens. The next stage is the selection meeting, where the range is shown to the merchandisers and heads of departments. The buyers present the garments for selection and the design team also contributes to the discussion about the range. The selection meeting takes place after the buyers have selected the garments to go into store and initial costings have been given by suppliers with achievable delivery dates. Joanna describes the purpose of the meeting and the preparation that is required:

> We have to do a lot of homework before a selection is made, and then the selection meeting is basically to inform the rest of the team – QC, merchandise and departmental heads: 'This is what we want to propose for autumn/winter 2001. We're proposing to put this tweed trouser with a certain supplier, and it will retail at £19.99 with this cost price, and this margin, which I think I can work on. We want to estimate about 8,000 pieces, and we want to put it in all-store distribution.' Then obviously in the selection meeting we would talk about the suitability of it going to all stores. 'Do we really think it's that commercial? Is it the right quantity and cost price?' QC would say: 'What's the cloth like? Have we used it before? Is the construction going to be too complicated, and could we bring the costs down by changing it?'

The selection meeting is attended by the buying and merchandise teams for woven, knit and jersey classics and the director of ladieswear (there is a separate selection meeting for the 'fashion' range). The classic range has already been fine-tuned by buying and design prior to this meeting, so its major purpose is to introduce the range to the merchandisers who can then assess order quantities, and to discuss any potential problems. The person responsible for making the distribution and the footage plan is invited to the selection meeting, as well as the visual merchandiser who might advise the buyers to amend the range depending on how it will be presented in store. Joanna describes selection as a 'constructive meeting', which provides an opportunity to assess how the products compare to the whole ladieswear range; for instance if there is a similar garment in another range at a different price, the cost of one of the styles needs to be renegotiated.

Once the range has been reviewed at selection and the whole team is satisfied with the garments the buying team is responsible for finalising the cost prices with suppliers. Merchandisers contact the suppliers to discuss the styles to be ordered, with quantities and delivery dates, followed by a booking fax to confirm this information. A 'new line sheet' is then generated for each style with a short product description, the fabric price, the colour, the garment's cost price and retail price, the components and the name of the supplier. New line sheets are issued to various departments for information to be inserted and the buyer's role is to describe the garment, its cost price, retail price, supplier and country of origin. The new line sheets have recently been transferred to a computerised system and sketches can be inserted by using a digital camera. Once a product has been signed off and the new line sheet completed, buyers request style confirmation sheets from the supplier, including the agreed cost price, size range, fibre composition, wash care instructions, additional wording such as 'Wash dark colours separately' and the expected delivery date. The buyer enters this information into the computer, then the merchandisers complete the contract before it is despatched to the supplier.

The buying team works on at least two seasons simultaneously, so during December they could be developing the garments for the following year's high summer range whilst the next autumn/winter range is at the initial concept stage. The George range is bought relatively closely to the season compared with other retailers, so they prefer to use suppliers who can operate a fairly quick turnaround for sampling and production of garments. The only supplier booked six months in advance by the womenswear team is based in Singapore, and production with other manufacturers can be booked after this. The lead time for the production of cloth from their suppliers is normally four weeks. The quickest methods of ordering cloth are to order greige cloth in advance or to buy cloth from stock, and it takes longer if the fabric is woven to order. The George buying team assess performance of the product area weekly on a 'this year/last year' (TYLY) basis. Each Monday a weekly sales report is distributed giving a breakdown of every product that is currently in store. They also have a weekly logbook of sales referred to as 'the bible' (introduced by George Davies). This lists how many units each style has sold, the profit, sales value, and the number of units remaining in the warehouse.

Supplier liaison

The suppliers for Joanna's product area are based in the UK, Cyprus and Turkey. She has not yet travelled to visit suppliers offshore though she has shadowed a buyer working with overseas garment suppliers on a visit to the UK. Joanna spends a high proportion of her working day liaising with garment manufacturers, which she views as one of the most enjoyable aspects of her job:

> *I think it's really important if you want to be a successful buyer to have a good rapport with suppliers. That way, you get respect from your suppliers, and of course you do your business better if they give you the production that you want and then you get the sales that you want.*

When negotiating prices with suppliers Joanna has a retail price in mind initially, then requests a first costing. After fitting the garment she discusses with the supplier any amendments required which may affect the cost price, like reducing the length of a skirt. Joanna always aims to meet the target margin, which she achieves 'nine times out of ten'.

Customers and market research

Buyers at GDP are encouraged to work in George retail outlets as often as possible, particularly on 'incentive days' when customers are offered 15 per cent off retail prices. Joanna participates in store visits as often as she can manage, which is up to six times a year:

> *I love to do that because, not only does it show that I'm understanding or learning more about promoting the garments on the shop floor ... but I also get to speak to the customers. I ask them what they like about George clothing and why they come here, so I get very direct customer feedback. The most memorable time was when I went to the opening of one of our biggest stores at the time, in Bristol, and a customer looking for a size 16 skirt told me: 'I really liked the tailored skirts, which used to come up to the knee. I always used to buy them because I found that I could wear them to go out in the evening and wear them at work'. That was such invaluable information because I had a meeting with the design team the next week where I said I'd found out that customers liked that length, so why didn't we reintroduce them? So we did a couple and the sales went through the roof.*

Other methods are used to gain feedback on the George range, including 'mystery callers' who pretend to be ordinary customers and ask shoppers for their opinions. A preview catalogue has been launched and sent to a limited mailing list of selected customers to assess reaction to new styles two months or more before delivery to stores. The quantities of garments ordered in bulk can be amended as a result of preview sales demand, or the styling of a garment may be altered to improve the sales potential.

Training and skills

Joanna has taken an in-house course on the buying department's computer system and is planning to participate in a negotiation course for buyers and merchandisers. She considers her experience in temping jobs (during summer holidays whilst at university) to have been 'invaluable':

> *I was quite fortunate to get six-week placements at head offices near my home, including British Aerospace and Diner's Club. That taught me how to interact with people in an office environment at different levels, how to talk on the phone to customers and to people in other businesses, faxing and software packages. I think the main thing I learned was speaking on the telephone, because you represent that company, regardless of who you speak to, and that is so important. It taught me how to get as much information as I could, and to be as efficient and polite as I could.*

Joanna considers computer skills to be important within her job though she would expect each company to provide in-house training on the software they use. Being able to type is also an advantage as she communicates regularly by e-mail and fax, with written confirmation being viewed within the company as the professional way in which to operate. Numeracy is required in Joanna's role and although profit margins can be calculated by computer, she also needs to be able to do this manually on a calculator. Before promotion to buyer level, staff at George are usually required to pass an internal exam to assess a variety of relevant skills.

Recruitment

GDP uses two main methods for recruiting assistant buyers. On the graduate training scheme successful applicants work in a store for a year, training as managers within the clothing department, before starting as assistant buyers at GDP. It is also possible to apply for an assistant buying job by applying for an advertised post or writing to Head Office, enclosing a CV. Interview candidates are invited to an assessment day, with up to 20 people participating in an individual interview, a group assessment, a tour around the office and a brief induction from each department. Sometimes there may be a separate second interview, involving a presentation to the interview panel. Joanna offers the following advice to those applying for a job as an assistant buyer:

Once you've got the job, I think the biggest shock you get in this type of role after joining from university is the hours. I usually work from 9 AM to 7 PM. When you're looking for a job, I wouldn't just go for how well-known the company is, but consider the location, as you're going to spend a lot of time there. Is there a town you can go to for your lunch hour? Are there catering facilities? Also, when you go for the interview, ask if you can walk around the office, as you get a sense of the atmosphere working there. If you can hear people laughing, you know you're on to a winner.

Future developments

An area which has recently been introduced at GDP is 'key entry price'. Key entry price means the most competitive retail prices that the buying team can possibly achieve, developed in response to competition from stores such as Matalan. Joanna expects this to be one of the most influential factors affecting the George range during 2001:

For January 2001, we're selling five-pocket Western jeans for £12 in two washes and three lengths, and long-sleeved jersey tops for £5. The key entry prices are all on the classic side of ladies' fashion, so this has been a whole project for me to work on ... but it's great because we're going to get so much promotion on it in stores. About every six weeks we'll introduce new colours of jersey tops or jeans, so we fill the range with low prices, but back it by high volume and keep the styles the same, whilst changing the colours to fit in with the season. It all started off from 'rollback' which was a big campaign that we did in conjunction with Asda, when they promoted to the customer: 'We're taking back our prices to two years ago'. We did it, and it worked.

The main developments at GDP during 2000 were the takeover of their parent company, Asda, by the American retailer, Wal-Mart, and the resignation of George Davies as chief executive. The impact of the Wal-Mart takeover has been relatively low-key; changes within the first six months have been limited to the installation of a new computer system at GDP and garments being stacked higher on the fitments within stores, thereby releasing more warehouse space. Buyers from Wal-Mart have visited the GDP headquarters and there is a possibility that the George range could be sold in other European countries and the USA.

Chapter 9
Mail Order Fashion Buying

Fashion buying for a mail order company is very similar to the buyer's role in a retail fashion multiple, but there are distinct differences in the way in which the products are sold, impacting upon range selection and sales figures. Listed below are some of the differences between buying for mail order and retail outlets:

- It is particularly important that garments are supplied on time or customers will be disappointed: in retail, customers may not realise if garments are out of stock.
- Garments cannot be touched or seen closely by the customer before they are ordered.
- Garments often vary in colour and quality from the catalogue photograph, due to printing processes, or because they have been made in different fabrics or by different suppliers.
- Sales per page and per catalogue are calculated as a measure of the range's performance.
- The garment returns rate is much higher in mail order than in retail, largely because customers may order several garments before making a purchase decision.

Mail order buyers follow the same buying cycle as in retail, as described in Chapter 3. The mail order buyer's job involves extra responsibilities in that they may be consulted during the compilation of the catalogue by other departments. After final selection the photo shoot takes place during the product development phase of the range, but the buyer is rarely able to make amendments since the garments already have been photographed. This can bring added pressure to the buyer's role and it is particularly important for the mail order buyer to be able to pay attention to detail and meet deadlines.

The mail order fashion market

Until the late 1980s, most mail order companies in the UK had a reputation for focusing on conservative garment designs at the cheaper end of the market.

Customers tended to work as agents by showing a catalogue such as Little-woods or Great Universal to friends, and earned a small commission on sales. As well as garments, the catalogues sold a wide variety of household merchandise. The products usually cost slightly more than comparable high street products but customers could spread out the payments over several months, enabling them to purchase goods which might otherwise be unobtainable to them. These so-called 'Big Book' catalogues still exist and are constantly updated to reflect a wide customer base, including sections which are bought as separate 'shops', ranging from young contemporary fashion to classic styles. Household goods, also referred to as hard goods, form a large section of these catalogues, containing products which are usually bought in a separate department from that of the fashion buying team.

The world's largest mail order company is Otto Versand, a private company based in Germany, which publishes catalogues throughout the world, including Spiegel (USA), Grattan (UK), Trois Suisses (France) and Otto (Germany). The UK's largest mail order company is Great Universal Stores (GUS), which also owns Argos, the high street catalogue store and the Burberry brand. Freemans catalogue is one of few to be based in London: most of the major UK catalogues are based in the North, including GUS (Manchester), Grattan (Bradford) and Empire (Leeds).

The development of Next Directory

The UK mail order market was revolutionised in 1988 with the launch of the Next Directory (see Figure 9.1). Next launched an innovative store concept and fashion product range in 1982, and the Next image had an impact on store design, visual merchandising and the co-ordination of other high street womenswear ranges. Next Directory had a similar effect on the mail order market by offering slick, minimal presentation and aspirational styling for menswear and womenswear. Most of the garments were the same as those sold through Next retail outlets, but the concept appealed to those with little time for shopping, particularly the continually-increasing number of working women. There were four major differences between the new Next Directory and the traditional Big Book catalogue:

(1) The Directory was hard-backed, giving it more of a desirable coffee-table book appearance. As a result, customers were asked to pay a cover charge of £3. Although this covered less than half of the actual cost, it made the catalogue seem more valuable and prestigious than its competitors.

(2) Delivery was promised within 48 hours by courier or post. The majority of merchandise was delivered on time, and usually more quickly than its

Figure 9.1 Page from the first edition of Next Directory 1988

competitors, many of whom subsequently reduced their delivery times. (Next now usually deliver products the following day.)
(3) Fabric swatches were included, to enable customers to see the colour and texture of the fabric. This system was later abandoned, as it was difficult to obtain sufficient bulk fabric at the publishing stage.
(4) Customers were not expected to operate as agents, and no commission was offered. A standard delivery charge was added to each order, rather than the 'free' delivery offered by competitors.

These factors combined with a commercial garment range, to give the Next Directory a more upmarket image than its predecessors. Mail order operations expertise was bought in by Next, by the merger with Grattan plc prior to the launch of the Next Directory. The success of the Next Directory is confirmed by the fact that the format remains largely unchanged, and Next continued to be a profitable concern during the late 1990s, at a time when many other established fashion retailers were suffering financially. Next products are now sold via retail outlets, mail order and the internet (www.next.co.uk), and garments from the catalogue can be delivered either to a home address or local store.

Recent entrants into the mail order fashion market

Possibly inspired by Next's success in this field, several fashion retailers have expanded into mail order, including French Connection Buy Mail and Principles. There are numerous specialist catalogues on a smaller scale than Next and the established 'big books'. Kingshill and The Book were launched in the 1990s, selling ready-to-wear and middle market womenswear ranges by mail order. Boden was founded by owner Johnnie Boden, selling men's, women's and children's classic fashion at upper mass market prices. In the twenty-first century, the mail order market is likely to expand considerably with the potential of new technologies, such as the internet, to effectively accommodate consumers' ever-changing lifestyles.

Compiling a catalogue

In addition to the selection of merchandise, there are numerous other processes involved in the compilation of a mail order catalogue, mostly relating to photography and publication. Buyers of mail order ranges are not likely to be involved directly with these processes but it is useful to be aware of them as they have an influence on product sales. The main processes are listed in Figure 9.2 and the roles which contribute to the compilation of the catalogue are explained below.

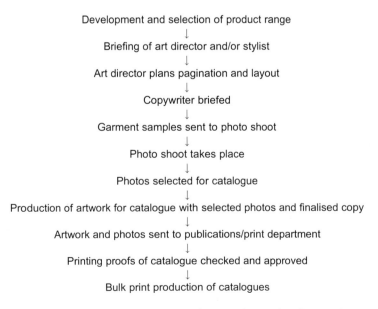

Development and selection of product range
↓
Briefing of art director and/or stylist
↓
Art director plans pagination and layout
↓
Copywriter briefed
↓
Garment samples sent to photo shoot
↓
Photo shoot takes place
↓
Photos selected for catalogue
↓
Production of artwork for catalogue with selected photos and finalised copy
↓
Artwork and photos sent to publications/print department
↓
Printing proofs of catalogue checked and approved
↓
Bulk print production of catalogues

Figure 9.2   Processes involved in the compilation of a mail order catalogue.

Art direction

It is the job of the art director to coordinate photographic shoots. Art directors are often freelance, as the job requires working for intermittent periods. Art directors have an equivalent role in mail order to that of visual merchandisers in retail fashion multiples. They have overall responsibility for the layout and image of the catalogue, which have a large influence on sales. The art director chooses the shoot location, models, stylist and photographer for the photographic shoot. The mail order buyer relies on the professionalism of the art director to enhance sales figures for the range. Buyers may have an opportunity to influence the shoot, and occasionally may attend. After the garment range has been finalised at the range presentation the fashion buyer usually briefs the art director, who sketches a plan of the layout of garment and text on the catalogue pages. This is known as pagination. The buying and/or design department may also be involved in the pagination of the range. The mail order fashion buyer can use pagination as the starting point for the planning of the range, with notes and/or sketches of the layout of each page and its contents, so that each item is seen in the context of the garments with which it will be displayed in the catalogue.

The buyer is responsible for ensuring that the right garments are sent to the photo shoot on time. This normally takes place before bulk garment production, so the garments worn by models are samples made in manufacturers' design departments. The fit of the garment will probably not have been approved at this stage, as photo shoots often take place within a very short timescale after the final range selection. The buyer may brief the art director and/or the stylist prior to the shoot, to explain the required look of each garment. Buyers attach a label to each garment containing relevant details such as reference numbers and any special instructions. This is one of the most hectic times of the season, and the buying team must support each other and pay great attention to detail: any mistakes made during a photo shoot are likely to be costly. The garments and relevant accessories are carefully packed into boxes by the buying team, to be sent to the photo shoot. Inevitably at least one garment arrives late, which may then need to be sent to the shoot by courier from the buying office or possibly directly from the manufacturer. This is acceptable for a small number of items if they are not planned for photography on the first day of the shoot, but it would be too costly for the whole range to be sent by courier.

Photography shoots usually take place in hot climates, to improve the chances of the clothes being photographed in good lighting conditions. Popular locations therefore include Florida and South Africa. Although the background scenery may barely be noticed by the catalogue customer, the weather has an effect on the appearance of the garments and models and the overall mood of the shot. There is however no absolute guarantee of good weather and shoots sometimes need to be extended at great cost due to adverse conditions, ranging from rain to hurricanes.

Fashion styling and photography

Most fashion stylists work on a freelance basis, and are responsible for achieving the appropriate image for the range at the photo shoot. This involves briefing the hairstylist and make-up artist, ensuring that the garment appears to fit correctly (often by using pins, sellotape and bulldog clips which are unseen in the photograph) and accessorising the models appropriately. During the photo shoot the team works closely together overseen by the art director. Polaroids are taken by the photographer before each shot, to give the art director an insight into how each photograph is likely to look, allowing changes to be made by the stylist and models if necessary. Photo shoots cost relatively large sums of money as they employ a team of highly-paid professionals (of which models and photographers are the most expensive) plus travel and accommodation. Several shots are taken of each pose, to allow the best image to be selected.

Selection of photographs

The photographs are developed as transparencies and then shown to the art director who makes a decision on the final shot to be used in the catalogue. The buyer may also be involved in the final selection of transparencies. This can be a difficult decision and requires a discerning eye as there are likely to be minor imperfections in many of the shots; the model's eyes may be partially closed or a key feature of the garment slightly obscured, which could result in lower sales. Some imperfections can be improved by the publications department by recolouring or deleting areas prior to the printing process. Digital photography and computer photo-editing programs may also allow the manipulation of images to achieve the desired effect.

Catalogue layout

It is important that the buyer has some say in the layout of the catalogue as the location and size of a photograph usually has a direct effect on sales figures. Garments on the right-hand page, products with large photographs and merchandise positioned in key positions such as the front or back cover or by the order form, usually have higher sales than products on left-hand pages or in small photographs, because the customer has higher exposure to these images. Yet if a garment is particularly appealing to the customer it will probably still sell well despite the photograph's size or location. Equally, inappropriate garments cannot be guaranteed higher sales even if the photographs are large.

Copywriting

The written details, or copy, displayed alongside the photographs in the catalogue, may be written either by the buyer, or a professional copywriter. The copy usually comprises a brief garment description, fibre content of the fabric, available sizes and selling price. Each catalogue has its own house style for copy including the typeface used and either basic or more descriptive garment details. Other written information is also likely to be required on each page, such as a name for the range, promotional information and brand logos for either garments or fabrics. The inclusion of the phone number for orders on the page is advantageous, even though it also appears on the order form and cover, as it makes ordering easier for the customer and can therefore increase sales. The art director receives the written information and images of the logos. After scanning in the final garment photos the art director can then use the computer to mock up the pages of the catalogue prior to printing. The buyer may be asked to check the pages at this stage, allowing any necessary adjustments to be made, such as selecting a different transparency or amending details of fibre content if necessary. The finished artwork is then passed to the publications department, who brief the printers. Copies of the pages at various stages in the printing process are submitted to the publications department, and the buyer may be responsible for checking the content.

Printing and publication

Mail order companies usually have a specialist publications department responsible for coordinating the printing of the catalogue after the layout has been designed and finalised by the art director. Various photographic and printing processes can distort colours from the originals. Photography shoots tend to take place in warm climates or in brightly-lit studios which can cause fabrics to look paler than they appear in natural daylight. Printing inks can also cause visible colour variations.

It is obviously important that catalogues show the colours of garments as realistically as possible to avoid disappointment from customers when they order the product. To ensure that the garments in the catalogue appear as close to the actual colour as possible, the publications department may request swatches of fabric or yarn for each style in the correct shade, prior to the catalogue being printed. The publications department may be responsible for checking colour-matching, or the buyer may be asked to approve initial prints of the catalogue in full colour (chromalins) by comparing them to swatches.

This usually takes place under the 'natural daylight' setting of a lightbox, which is kept in a darkened room to avoid contamination from other sources of light.

Assessing the sales performance of a mail order range

There are several ways of showing sales figures for mail order. They can be calculated either through financial turnover, total *price* of garments sold, or the total *number* of garments sold. A garment costing £50 which has sold 1000 pieces has a higher sales turnover (£50,000) than one costing £20 which has sold 2000 pieces (£40,000).

The gross sales figure for a style is the total number of garments ordered by customers multiplied by its selling price. The net sales figure denotes gross sales minus returns, showing orders which have resulted in garments being kept by customers, and is therefore the most important indicator of the sales performance of a mail order range.

The rate of returns is relatively high in mail order, often in excess of 50 per cent of orders, largely due to customers having ordered a selection of goods and deciding which ones to keep upon receipt. Customers may simply have changed their minds on receiving the garments, or ordered several garments with the intention of buying only the best ones. Many returns are due to quality and fit. For example upon inspection the make-up quality may not be of the standard expected by the customer, the colour may vary from the printing in the catalogue and the garment proportion may not reflect the image shown in the original photograph. This calculation can be applied either to individual garments or to a complete range:

$$\text{Gross sales value} - \text{Total value of returns} = \text{Net sales}$$

Calculating profit as a percentage of net sales gives senior managers the opportunity to compare like-for-like sales between buyers, using the following formulae:

$$\text{Net sales} - \text{total cost price of goods} = \text{Gross margin}$$

$$\frac{\text{Net sales} - \text{Total cost price of goods}}{\text{Net sales}} \times 100 = \text{Percentage gross margin}$$

Buying for the internet

By 2000 many fashion retailers had set up websites initially mainly for promotional purposes. Selling products via an internet website is known as e-commerce and companies which operate transactional websites are referred to as e-tailers. Many mail order companies sell via the internet as well as through catalogues since the two methods of distribution are complementary, based on selling from photographs, stocking merchandise at a central location and postal delivery. Next is currently the UK's largest on-line clothing retailer. The Arcadia Group plc launched its 'Zoom' website in 1999, as an internet portal, offering products from its retail fascias: Top Shop, Top Man and Principles. This was promoted by offering free CD-Roms via its retail outlets, with free internet access. Boo.com, an e-tailer specialising in branded fashion goods, was launched in a blaze of publicity in 1999, and was the victim of an equally well-publicised demise in 2000 when the company's financial backers withdrew their funds. With increasing access to the internet and a governmental policy of encouraging wider ownership of computers, the internet is likely to become one of the major methods of distributing fashion merchandise in the near future, following similar development processes to those used for mail order.

Summary

Buying a fashion range for mail order is largely similar to buying for a retailer, with only a few key differences. GUS, Littlewoods and Next are some of the major mail order fashion companies in the UK. After final range selection, the following processes take place in the compilation of a catalogue:

- Handover of sample garments to art directors and stylists
- Planning of the catalogue's layout by the art director
- Photo shoot
- Selection of photos for the catalogue
- Finalisation of catalogue layout
- Printing of catalogues

Net sales figures are used to assess the sales performance of a mail order range. Buying for the internet is similar to buying for mail order, and this is expected to become a more popular method of selling fashion merchandise.

Case studies in mail order fashion buying

Boden

Fiona is senior buyer for womenswear at Boden, the mail order fashion company. After taking A-levels in English, History and French, Fiona graduated in 1986 with a BSc in textile technology, specialising in management. She started as a trainee buyer at Debenhams, where she worked for nine years, before moving to the buying department at Richards. Fiona joined Boden in 1998 as a senior buyer.

The company's clothing catalogue was launched in 1991 by Johnnie Boden, a former stockbroker. He was inspired while working in New York by American retail and mail order companies for the 30-something customer. He decided to change career completely by establishing a similar type of mail order company in the UK, on a much smaller scale, developing clothes which would appeal to him and his friends. He started with a menswear range, and introduced womenswear three years later, followed by the Mini Boden childrenswear range and, more recently, Baby Boden.

Roles and responsibilities

Fiona's buying team includes a junior buyer who is responsible for part of the range, and an assistant buyer. Fiona also oversees two garment technicians and a design technician, who organises patterns and sample garments. The merchandiser and assistant merchandiser on the womenswear area report directly to the merchandise director. There are separate buying teams for menswear, childrenswear and accessories. (The head designer for womenswear is also responsible for overseeing parts of the Mini Boden and accessories areas.) A designer with specific responsibility for all of the knitwear reports to the head designer, and there is an assistant designer working solely on womenswear. Boden also employ a menswear designer, a childrenswear designer and an accessories designer. Fiona's role involves liaison with a number of departments within the company:

Figure 9.3   Structure of the buying department at Boden.

My main link is with design obviously, travelling together, and putting the range together. Being a mail order company, we're very involved with marketing, on the photographic side, and how the catalogue's going to look, and how things will be shot. I liaise a lot with the other buying departments – menswear, childrenswear and accessories, on fabrics and suppliers. I have contact on a more ad hoc *basis with the warehouse, customer services and finance.*

It is Fiona's responsibility as a senior buyer to control the development of the womenswear range from initial ideas through to featuring products in the catalogue and beyond. She starts planning a range by looking at styles that have sold well in the past, which are then updated, and by looking at current trends and new ideas with the design team. She is also heavily involved in sourcing garments, deciding on which factories to place styles with, as well as sourcing fabrics and negotiating prices. Fiona's main tasks include range planning and selection, mainly in conjunction with designers and merchandisers. She also briefs the marketing team, helping to specify how the products will be photographed, how she wants garments to be shown in the catalogue, and relevant information about the products. In addition to developing the main catalogue ranges, Fiona is involved in developing garments which help to promote the Boden brand in the press:

In terms of promotion, at the beginning of the season, if we know a particular magazine wants to use our products, such as Red Direct, *we'll develop products for them which are based on items from the range, but not identical. Promotion for Boden is often through magazine articles. We've done inserts in* Good Housekeeping *and* Country Living, *which are the most popular magazines with our customers. We have worked in the past with the* Sunday Times *and the* Sunday Telegraph. *Generally, the magazines and newspapers will approach us to work on projects with them.*

Another area of Fiona's responsibility is maintaining quality standards and ensuring that garments fit correctly by liaising with the QC team, who look at returns information, comments from customers and sealing samples. The QC team checks garments during production, and inspects garments which have been delivered to the warehouse. Fiona also oversees in-season management of the stock with the merchandiser, deciding which styles require repeat orders and where they will be sourced. She describes some of the varying elements of the senior buyer's role:

The parts of the job which I enjoy most are creating ideas and planning the range, then managing that throughout the season and reacting to it. You get a buzz from the sales and reacting to the bestsellers, particularly when you have to buy more. There are no two days the same. You can come in in the morning with a list of things to do and by the end of the day not have achieved any of it, but have had a jam-packed day doing other things. Because I'm a buyer and manager, one of the most difficult things is having to do the job and make sure that a lot of other people are doing what they should be doing as well. Probably the most difficult thing is juggling priorities and getting everything done, and remaining calm while all of this is going on. When I started here, there was jargon that I'd never heard of: there's buying-specific jargon, but each company has its own jargon as well.

Fiona describes her role as a buyer/manager, as she develops ideas with design, plans and books the range whilst overseeing and managing her garment technicians and assistant buyers, ensuring that they keep to the critical path.

The buying cycle

At the same time that the range for one season is being launched to customers, the buyers are about to book business for the next season, and the designers are working on initial ideas for the following season. At Boden, the buying cycle commences with directional shopping trips and visits to trade fairs such as *Première Vision*. The information from these trips is exchanged between the buyers and designers at an initial ideas meeting.

At the beginning of the season the buying team starts range planning with a historical analysis of key lines, which are garments that run for several seasons and are frequently updated. The merchandiser reviews the range from a numerical point of view, based on previous sales, and breaks down the overall budget into product categories, such as trousers or shirts. The buyers and designers identify new trends which they consider to be appropriate for the Boden customer. It is important for Fiona to decide carefully which fashion trends to include within the range: 'Our customers are aware of fashion, but they don't want to look ridiculous. We've got to decide if those trends are relevant, and how we interpret them.'

An inital selection meeting is convened when all of the garment samples have been developed by suppliers. This is followed by final selection meetings with the company's directors. Initial selection meetings for womenswear at Boden can be up to two days long, and final selection usually takes one day. The womenswear range is finalised and signed off in December for the following autumn/winter, then orders for the styles are placed with the suppliers. Shortly afterwards the buying team gives a full presentation of the range to the in-house art director and marketing team. Buyers run through the whole concept behind the range in detail, product by product, including how they would like the garments to be shot and in which type of environment, enabling the art director to plan the pagination of the catalogue. Fiona refers to the next stage as 'outfitting':

> I might say: 'We want to shoot that top in that colour, with that trouser in that colour, with those shoes and that bag'. We have a computerised system for product development, so everything we do at each stage is being input into this system, and it means that as we're putting the range together we can say 'this would look really good if we shot it in this way' and input our ideas as we go along. The marketing team have creative input into the photographic shoot, but there's quite a rigid basis from which they work.

Some of the photographs are shot in the UK, and designers may occasionally attend, but the marketing team takes the main responsibility for this area. A copy meeting takes place after the handover to the marketing department, as there is a strong emphasis on the written copy about products in the Boden catalogue. Johnnie Boden and the buying team have a substantial amount of input into this.

Once a range has been launched, key performance indicators (KPIs) are used on a company-wide basis to review its success. This involves reviewing net sales figures, which is how much customers actually purchase, and demand, which is how much people initially order. Boden have a target of 85% fill-rate, which refers to the amount of items that are in stock when customers place orders.

Supplier liaison

Inevitably, Fiona's job involves travelling on directional shopping trips and supplier visits:

> On the shopping side, we have trips to Paris and New York. We're talking about going to LA and a bit further afield in Europe. I go to Hong Kong, Portugal and Morocco on garment sourcing trips. We do a lot of jerseywear and a few woven garments in Portugal. Hong Kong is mainly knitwear, as

well as some casualwear, such as washed cotton, cord and moleskin. Morocco is mainly trouser production, but we're beginning to develop a bit more there.

I don't source much womenswear in the UK, though they do on the accessories side. We deal with UK suppliers who have production offshore, in Morocco and Poland. We are trying to look more into buying from the UK, with a few factories on the knitwear side, but unfortunately the way the industry's gone, they're going out of business and it's really difficult. There are a few factories in the UK that I'm looking at for specific areas, but it does come down to the product and the cost. Customers aren't prepared to pay more and more for their garments and we've got to be realistic, but also we've got the state of the British textile industry against us in that where we've tried, it's been very difficult, and it's something that we're conscious of. On womenswear, there are certain areas, like tweeds, where we buy English fabric, and though the garments are not necessarily all made up in the UK, it's something we're trying to look at, so we can promote the British side a bit more. For somebody like us, we're slightly more upmarket and we can pay a bit more for our products, we deal with better fabrics, and we're probably better placed to deal with some of the UK people.

Fiona considers the potential flexibility of UK suppliers to be an advantage, for example she has bought knitwear from Hong Kong in large quantities, but because Boden is mail order and needs a quick response in-season, she has tried using UK production for repeat orders. Fiona explains some of the criteria used in selecting suppliers for garment production:

Suppliers have strengths in producing certain products. We look at the size of the company. Boden has come from a very small base, and we have a lot of small suppliers. The accessories department may use people who've been producing jewellery for a stand in Spitalfields Market, but their product can be very relevant to Boden. On a bigger scale, if I'm buying 6,000 units (of a style) in a season, I want somebody who can cope with it, who knows the product, can give me the service, be flexible in terms of booking everything up front. It has to be somebody who can produce the quality that we require. Price comes into it, but we're probably not as price-sensitive as a lot of people.

Customers and market research

Boden's marketing department is pro-active in gaining feedback from customers by sending questionnaires with catalogues on a yearly basis. Customers who have not bought from the company within that time may receive letters asking for suggestions on how Boden could regain their custom. Fiona and her team are given information about customers from the marketing department:

> *Customers are demanding more, they're more aware of price, but also where things are made. Trying to get a balance between the two is difficult. We have boards with customer profiles up around the building, with names, and what they do. Johnnie set Boden up for himself and his friends initially, which is the underlying customer profile.*

Training and skills

Boden employ a training coordinator to organise relevant in-house courses. Fiona describes the importance of numeracy and computer skills within the buying role:

> *As we do product development on the computer, it's the most computer-skilled place I've worked at, and probably most companies are going that way, especially with email, etc. When you're doing negotiations and planning, it's all very numerical.*

Recruitment

Boden usually advertise for buying vacancies. When drafting interview short-lists from CVs, they look for computer skills and numeracy. Interviewers aim to ascertain how well applicants work in a team, how they deal with problems or difficult situations, and also ask them questions specific to the company, such as what they know about Boden. Interviewees for buying jobs may be asked where they shop for clothes, who they think the potential customer is, and which companies are direct competitors, to establish whether they would fit into the Boden environment. It is not essential for applicants to have previous mail order experience, though some knowledge about how mail order differs from retail may be advantageous. A personnel department has recently been established at Boden, where CVs of applicants are kept on file. Fiona plays an active role in the recruitment of buying staff:

> *Recently, when we were recruiting assistants, personnel came straight to me and my director to sift through the CVs, and he did the first interviews. I was in a selection meeting, so I did the second interview. We look for somebody who's got a degree or relevant background. If somebody had left school at 16 but had worked in relevant places and wanted to come here, we wouldn't discount them. I would advise anyone thinking of starting a career in buying that when I was at school everyone thought it was this fantastically glamorous job, and it certainly isn't. They've got to be prepared for very hard*

work and be very flexible. Every day is different, you're constantly having to juggle priorities and you've got to be prepared to work with that. Also it can be long hours if you've got meetings to prepare for, but I don't know if that's any different to other industries. The upside is you can be working with really nice product and you get discount! And once you get to buyer level, although the foreign trips are hard work (particularly when you can spend six hours travelling into China and back from Hong Kong in one day to spend a day at a factory) I still do consider myself lucky to go to these countries, although you don't get time to sightsee. However, summer holidays in Cornwall are becoming more appealing!

Future developments

Fiona attributes Boden's current success partly to the fact that it is a mail order company, making it ideally placed to benefit from e-commerce:

Technology is going to have a positive effect on us, because we are getting more sales from the internet. More people are getting into buying clothing by mail order, which is also positive. Boden has a different 'handwriting'. You don't always get what we do anywhere else in the high street, because we design in-house. Retail itself is struggling badly at the moment, but we are getting more and more new customers.

Next

This case study centres on a buying manager for Next plc within the childrenswear department. She took a BTEC National Diploma and Higher National Diploma which were followed by a first job as a trainee buyer for a jeanswear retailer. Her first job at Next was as a trainee buyer for both formal and casual men's shirts for 18 months, then as an assistant buyer for another 18 months before being promoted to buyer. After three years, she left the business to work for a menswear competitor before returning to Next to buy mens's jerseywear, sportswear and resortwear. After a spell on womenswear, she then transferred to girlswear within the childrenswear department where she has remained for the last two years.

Roles and responsibilities

Product director

↑

Buying manager

↑

Buyer

↑

Assistant buyer

↑

Trainee buyer

Figure 9.4   Structure of the Next buying department.

Due to the coordinated nature of the childrenswear range, the designers, buyers and merchandisers must work closely together and the teams are physically located together within the same building. The buying team also interface with other departments within the business, such as marketing and sales. For mail order, the product team have a Directory coordinator who, together with the buyers, gives direction on product content for each page to the Directory creative & production team. There is a main book Directory and a brochure each season and occasionally some shots need to be changed before publication. The buying department would be involved in these decisions. This may occur if a line is cancelled or if the team do not feel the picture works.

The buying manager plans the overall strategy of the girlswear range and manages the team. She has overall responsibility for the styling, pricing and profitability of the girlswear range and must ensure that both the product and pricing sit well within the rest of the childrenswear collection. The buying manager looks at the whole picture whereas buyers are focusing on their individual product types. Often the greatest challenge is managing the personnel side of the job and being exposed to some of the problems that other people have. A good team is very important as the Next buying manager explains:

The buying cycle

The buying team usually work on three seasons simultaneously for most of the year. The new season starts with travel to some of the world's major cities for ideas and inspiration, together with some of the designers. On their return the designers put together their forecasts in terms of colours, themes, the looks and developments for key selling areas. Budgets, margins and average selling prices are planned at the range direction meeting together with any proposed changes to the supply base. Planning for new ranges starts about a year in advance of the on-sale date.

After range direction, the designers then work on designing specific styles which, after discussion with buyers and technologists, are issued to suppliers in design packs. Over the next few weeks, the suppliers will make samples from the design packs for buyers, designers and technologists to view together with prices. On visits to these suppliers by Next, amendments and re-sampling will be done as required.

Back at head office, the samples are collated and the styles are then reviewed as a range. A rangebuilding meeting is held where the team assesses all the styles and estimates their sales potential, placing them in order of rank. Pre-selection meetings then follow where the merchandisers and buyers present the range, margins and pricing to the childrenswear product director. This can be a very detailed meeting with discussions on fabrics, fit and manu-facturers. After a period of around three weeks a final selection meeting takes place when the buyers have had the opportunity of obtaining more finalised samples, which may have been amended since pre-selection. Fabrics and styles are agreed at this meeting and orders are then raised on the compu-terised system over the next two weeks. Point-of-sale (POS) tickets together with the presentation and packaging requirements are then raised through the system and forwarded to the manufacturer. Buyers, merchandisers and technologists are responsible for various different factors in the product development process but it is the buyer who is ultimately responsible for progressing the order through from the initial sample to production.

The deliveries are received into Next's UK warehouse and then on to the stores or to Next Directory customers. The buyer monitors sales to identify repeat orders and customer spending patterns. Sales are monitored and assessed on a weekly basis. Sales from the Next Directory Preview catalogue help the buyers and merchandisers to forecast sales for stores and the hardback Directory, which is issued three months later. The childrenswear buying manager travels regularly within her job to locations including New York, Hong, Tokyo, Portugal and Paris as well as in the UK. It is very hard work and can be a tiring experience. It is not necessarily as glamorous as it sounds.

Supplier liaison

The buying manager looks for new suppliers to help develop her product area and supply base. Prospective suppliers are checked over for their manufacturing capabilities, production capacity and quality standards, such as broken needle and metal detector policies, which are particularly important for childrenswear. Other retailers serviced by the supplier are also taken into account. If the buying manager is satisfied that this prospective supplier has potential, a Next technologist will visit the factory and carry out a thorough audit including Next's code of practice.

Customers and market research

Various sources of market research are available to the buying teams at Next. The marketing department commissions market research, both internally and externally, and gives feedback to the buyers. They also listen carefully to their customers through visits to our stores, the customer services department and information from Next Directory returns. This enables them to stay focused on giving their customers what they want.

Training and skills

Most of the training for trainee buyers is on the job, which is the responsibility of the buyer, but Next does have a comprehensive training manual and buying school to teach specific buying techniques. Next provides in-house training such as computer skills, time management and presentation skills. Numeracy and computer skills are important, in conjunction with other abilities. Trainee buyers spend a considerable amount of time on the computer, as orders are systems-generated. The company uses email extensively, so good keyboard skills are definitely a bonus. Although numeracy skills will make the administrative part of the job easier, they certainly do not by themselves make someone a buyer, because a buyer also needs to be able to put a range together. When trainee buyers get their cost prices now, they key them into the computer and it generates the landed price, whereas it used to be done manually. Numeracy is definitely needed, but it is not the first requirement.

Recruitment

Initially, applicants for trainee buyer posts at Next undertake an aptitude and numeracy test. If they pass this test, they are invited to an assessment day to participate in an interview and a group discussion and to give a presentation on a topic. They are then given a range presentation exercise and asked to rank some styles from one to ten and to explain the reasons for these rankings. The buying manager and her buyers participate in the interview process for trainee buyers. The recruitment process is quite tough, and as well as human resources (HR), the buying team get involved. There is quite a structured interview process with all of the interviewees being interviewed by HR and buying, so everyone is asked the same questions and marked in the same way, so it's quite fair. The interviewer needs to know if a trainee buyer has a flair for range building, so that they ultimately will have the skills and ability to progress to buyer, and this is very difficult to access. For a clothing product, if applicants don't have that flair, they can't learn it. They can't read a book and say: 'Oh yes, I can do that now'.

Applicants for buying positions are expected to be reasonably numerate and also committed, because the hours can be quite long. The working hours in the Next buying department are officially 9 to 5, but it is not unusual for people to arrive at work around 8am and leave at 6pm or even later. A trainee buyer would need to have a certain amount of creativity, but to be commercial with it. They wouldn't be expected to know the market in great detail, but to have an understanding of it. Buyers need someone who is quite flexible, because they might have quite a structured day to start with, but things change and they have to adapt. Trainee buyers need to persevere and push themselves forward as it is a competitive environment, but the rewards are definitely worth it. Generally speaking it takes four or five years to progress from trainee buyer to buyer. Buyers handle multi-million pound budgets so the company needs to be sure applicants are ready for that job role. People who love it will get totally immersed in it – they need to be passionate about the whole thing.

Future developments

It will be interesting to see how the high street changes in the near future and the consequent effect on Next. The development of the internet will also affect shopping patterns, although it is felt that it will not replace shopping in stores.

Chapter 10
Buying Branded Fashion Merchandise

This chapter concentrates on buying for stores that sell mainly branded fashion merchandise. Although some of these stores develop their own products, the emphasis of the buying role is on selecting finalised styles which have already been designed by other companies and therefore are sold with branded names rather than under the shop's own label. Most of these stores are independent companies who do not belong to large retail parent companies, and have a small number of outlets, from one to approximately 20 branches. Browns in London and Pollyanna in Barnsley are included amongst the most well-known stores in the UK selling branded fashion merchandise. Most department stores develop their own ranges, such as the Jonelle range in John Lewis and the J. Taylor range in Debenhams, as well as buying branded fashion merchandise with different buying teams working on separate ranges. Department stores may sell several fashion brands alongside each other or as individual concessions (see Chapter 8).

The owners of independent stores often undertake the buying role along with numerous other tasks. They rarely employ merchandisers so this becomes the buyer's responsibility. Larger independent stores employ specialist buyers who will usually have a background in retail management. There is less need in this type of job for qualifications or experience in fashion design than there is in a buying position for a chain store, since there is unlikely to be any design or product development involved in the role. It is more important that the buyer is familiar with the store's customers and their requirements, and it is much easier in this type of store for the buyer to gain a first-hand view of the clientele. The buying job for an independent store may be combined with a sales role within the shop particularly if there is only one outlet, as the buying role may not warrant a full-time salary. Buying fashion products for an independent store is different from buying non-fashion merchandise (see Figure 10.1) as it is essential that the buyer is able to select the right merchandise for the season and sell garments within a precise time-frame; the ability to gauge the right product at the right time is even more important in this field.

Budget planning and ordering merchandise

The buying role for branded merchandise often involves budget planning for future seasons and monitoring the budget for the current season. The buyer needs to predict how much money should be spent on a season's merchandise, and they must factor into the equation how much was sold last season, the constraints of space within the store (and therefore the number of garments which can be accommodated) and the amount of money which the company has available to spend.

Most merchandise is ordered well in advance but the buyer needs to retain a certain portion of money to buy goods within the season itself – this is known as 'open-to-buy'. With this money, which could be approximately 10 per cent of the whole season's budget, the buyer has a safety net in case a key trend is missing from the range or if there is an opportunity to buy goods at a discounted price. Most of the merchandise bought from the open-to-buy budget will usually be purchased from stock, that is products which have already been manufactured and can be delivered almost immediately. Occasionally stock merchandise can be bought at a special price particularly towards the end of a season, as the brand needs to sell it quickly to recover its costs before it is out of date. Mid-season trade fairs, aimed mostly at the home market, are held in several countries. These benefit buyers who have sold the season's range well and need some replacement styles, and buyers of branded labels who wish to sell ranges more frequently than twice per year. When planning budgets buyers need to take account of the fact that not all of the merchandise will be sold at full price and some garments will inevitably be marked down at the end of the season, thereby reducing the profits on some styles.

Selecting ranges of branded fashion merchandise

Buyers for independent stores usually visit showrooms to view ranges of branded fashion merchandise. Some buyers travel abroad to do this, typically visiting cities like Milan, Paris and London, where many fashion brands show at trade fairs and have showrooms. Trade fairs such as the SEHM menswear show in Paris or Pure womenswear show in London have the advantage of exhibiting a wide selection of brands in the same place, allowing buyers to see many ranges within a short period, and identifying potential new brands to stock. Some buyers may visit fabric trade fairs such as *Première Vision* in Paris even though they are not involved in fabric selection as this will give them an early preview of forthcoming fabric and colour trends up to six months ahead of the buying period for the season. Buyers from many stores are likely to visit the same locations during peak buying periods, offering them an opportunity to

Budget planning
↓
Planning buying schedules and trips
↓
Range selection
↓
Price negotiation and retail price-setting
↓
Processing orders
↓
Order confirmation
↓
Monitoring deliveries
↓
Monitoring sales figures
↓
Reviewing the season's performance

Figure 10.1   The buying cycle for branded fashion merchandise.

network. As most independent stores are not in direct competition with each other, being based in different towns and cities, a camaraderie may be built up between buyers from different stores, who will often share information on the performance of brands.

Some of the brands, particularly the higher priced designer ready-to-wear labels, present their ranges at runway shows, to which buyers who are current or potential customers may be invited. Although catwalk shows were originally created as a method of showing new garment ranges to buyers they are now targeted primarily at the media with the press taking priority over buyers in the seating arrangements. This situation should be welcomed by buyers as increased press coverage can mean higher sales for stockists of the brand. Some of the most prestigious brands are extremely selective about stockists for their products and will only sell to those who meet their own strict criteria. This is the reverse of the usual situation for the buyer who is used to having the upper hand when selecting which brands to stock. Those who are fortunate enough to be accepted by the major brands can find that profit margins and sales are relatively low for these labels, but they are worth stocking to tempt in extra customers who actually purchase lower-priced merchandise but are attracted by the kudos of famous names. At the opposite end of the spectrum, brands with street-cred which are known more through word-of-mouth than advertising or catwalk shows can enhance the image of the store. The buyer needs to have a thorough knowledge of the customer's lifestyle and culture to be able to spot such brands. The following list includes examples of fashion brands, classified by product and customer type:

- Surf/skatewear brands for the younger menswear and womenswear market: Mambo, O'Neill, Quiksilver.
- Contemporary casual menswear and womenswear: Boxfresh, Diesel, Firetrap.
- Upper middle market womenswear brands: Escada, Feminella, Mondi.

Buyers for independent stores need to review on a seasonal basis which brands should be stocked to offer a mix of labels to appeal to the store's customer base. This decision will be based largely on sales figures which must be taken within the context of other factors such as reliability and service from the brand, weather conditions and brand awareness. A brand which has performed poorly in its first season in a store should not necessarily be discarded as the buyer may need to review the selling prices or may have confidence in the label being the next big thing. The buyer should be aware of the amount of promotion undertaken by the brand as this could have a significant impact on sales, particularly if a specific garment is due to be featured in an advertising campaign and is likely to be requested by customers. Independent fashion stores tend to target the middle to higher price bracket where the kudos created by the label can be as important as the styling features of the garment.

Retail price setting for branded merchandise

Branded fashion suppliers have set prices for the garments within their ranges. These may be negotiable depending on the total volume of merchandise that the customer is buying, how long the store has been a stockist of the range, and the time of year, as brands may be keen to clear out stock towards the end of a season. The buyer is responsible for setting retail prices, which are usually two to three times the cost price from the manufacturer in this sector of the market (a lower mark-up, on average, than the mark-up used by the larger high street chains). The buyer aims to have a target mark-up (or margin) throughout the range, but this is calculated as an average, allowing the buyer the flexibility to make a higher percentage of profit on some styles and less on others, where appropriate. The mark-up on the range needs to cover all of the overheads of running the store/s including such factors as rent, utility bills, wages, advertising and promotion, whilst retaining a profit for the owners or shareholders. Cashflow can often be a problem for smaller fashion retailers, particularly when launching a first store. Payment for the merchandise has to be made shortly after delivery from the supplier but the store will not generate income until some time later during the subsequent weeks and months when customers begin to purchase the garments. For this reason an independent store may need to include loan payments as an overhead to help finance the business, and a new store would be unlikely to make a profit for at least the first year.

Processing orders and monitoring deliveries

Having seen the new season's range several months before delivery, buyers order garments either in the showroom or from their own offices. Waiting a few days to finalise orders is wise as the buyer will have had the chance to see several ranges and to make decisions which are more appropriate than those made during a showroom visit. The buyer then has an opportunity to discuss garments with sales staff, who may be able to offer a more commercial perspective.

Most independent retailers have their own system of paperwork to complete when ordering products (see Figure 10.2). The order sheets are submitted to the salespeople at the brand's office, detailing the style reference, colour, fabric, number of pieces, size ratio and expected delivery date. A buyer for an independent store buys smaller volumes than most department stores and needs to decide how many garments should be bought per size, as there is unlikely to be equal demand in each size. In a large chain store, the merchandiser usually takes responsibility for this but, for a smaller independent store it is part of the buyer's role.

For a store ordering ten garments per style the following size ratio could be specified by the buyer:

Size:	8	10	12	14	16	18
Quantity:	1	1	2	3	2	1

The quantities in a size ratio can be expressed either as numbers or percentages. The ratio selected by the buyer will depend on previous sales history and how appropriate the style is considered to be for larger sizes. Typically, a short, fitted style may only be purchased in smaller sizes, but buyers could potentially increase sales by reconsidering stereotypes. Size 18 customers might actually be keen to buy such a style, since other retailers may be reluctant to take the risk of stocking it. Independent retailers need to regularly review their size ranges which may alter gradually each year. Selecting the right range of sizes is a crucial decision as sales will obviously be lost if there are insufficient garments in a particular size, leaving disappointed customers with a negative impression of the store.

This system is referred to as forward ordering, as garments are usually delivered several weeks or months after the order date. Manufacture of the garments often does not begin until initial orders have been made by customers, enabling the branded company to anticipate the quantity per style to be produced. However orders are not always on schedule and are sometimes incomplete. It is advisable to anticipate that some garments will arrive later than requested and the buyer will inevitably need to chase up progress on delivery

Company		Department	Psyche Ltd. Buyer	ORDER No.	201-203 + 215 Linthorpe Road MIDDLESBROUGH TS1 4AU Tel: 01642 888333 Fax: 01642 221057
		Women ☐	Company rep.	0051	

Season _____

Date _____

Today's Exchange Rate £1 =

Tel: _____

Delivery dates _____

PSYCHE®

Women's Clothing Purchase Order

www.psyche.co.uk

Style Name/No.	Fabric content	Colour	Size Scale												TOTAL	Description	Cost (Ex VAT)	Retail Price
			E			6	8	10	12	14	16	18		8				
			F	2	3	3H	4	4H	5	5H	6	6H	7	7H				
			G				XS	S	M	L	EL							
			H	24	26	27	28	29	30	31	32	33	34				
			J					ONE									

Figure 10.2 Psyche order sheet.

with some suppliers. To pre-empt problems, the buyer might request an earlier delivery date than necessary, if the store has sufficient storage space. Another contingency plan could be to order slightly more stock than required from the more reliable companies, though the buyer needs to be confident that this merchandise can be sold profitably. When the garments arrive, the buyer will need to complete the relevant paperwork to log delivery and compare this with the order sheets, to check that the merchandise is correct.

Monitoring sales figures and reviewing the season's performance

The buyer is likely to meet regularly with the store manager to gain feedback on sales figures and anecdotal information from customers. If a style is not selling well the sales staff may be able to tell the buyer some of the comments that customers have made about it. This is a distinct advantage of buying for this type of store as feedback is immediate and detailed which allows the buyer to understand any problems with garments and respond quickly to customer feedback. Equally the buyer also needs to be prepared to accept that if a mistake has been made in selecting a garment for the range, he or she will know about it very quickly. Weekly reports on sales figures are usually compiled by sales staff and can even be made available on a daily basis, allowing the buyer to review the range's performance constantly. The buyer can then decide whether to act by ordering extra merchandise to replace styles that are selling quickly or reduce the price of garments which are moving too slowly. Buyers predict the amount of sell-through required of the range within a season, which means the amount of stock sold at full price prior to sale markdowns. Pre-sale sell-through can be predicted separately for each brand stocked within the store as the buyer might expect certain brands to have stronger sales figures than others, depending on the customer's taste and life style.

Repeat orders and markdowns

Stores often work to a target of 10 or 12 weeks' cover, meaning that they aim to sell out of a garment style within this period. If 10 pieces of a style have been bought but only one has been sold within four weeks, the buyer would estimate this garment to take another 36 weeks to sell out (nine garments selling at the rate of one every four weeks) which is obviously such a long time that it would still be on sale in the next season. Action therefore needs to be taken and the buyer would probably aim to mark it down early in the season to recoup as much money as possible rather than waiting to reduce it even further in the sale. This decision needs to be taken in the light of many other factors including the weather, which obviously has a major and often unpredictable effect on sales figures. A buyer might expect sales of swimwear to start slowly in the spring season but be prepared to wait for the weather to improve before considering a price reduction. Some independent retailers including Psyche, offer financial incentives such as bonuses to buyers to encourage them to make commercially sound decisions.

PR and promotion

The buyer for an independent store invariably has a wider role than a chain-store buyer and this can often extend to public relations (PR) and promotion for the company. Many independent fashion retailers advertise in the local press, particularly during sale periods. Some independents keep a database of customers' names and addresses and send a direct mailshot such as a postcard or invitation, at key times of the year often offering discounts during a certain period. This can boost customer loyalty and help build up more of a relationship between the store and customers. As the customer has voluntarily left their personal details this can result in a higher response than would be expected from an unsolicited mailshot.

Some independent stores organise fashion shows for their customers as a promotional exercise. They may be held in-store in the evening by invitation only, or at an alternative venue. This can increase customer loyalty particularly if clients have been personally invited and a discount is offered for orders placed at the event. Apart from benefiting the customer the discount may be useful to the store if the fashion show is held at the beginning of the season as it offers an insight into which styles are likely to sell well, allowing the buyer to plan orders effectively. Fashion shows can be too expensive for most independent retailers as they cost several thousands of pounds if professional models, choreographers, sound and lighting systems are used.

Summary

Buying branded fashion merchandise for independent retailers or department stores differs from buying for retail fashion multiples in that the buyer is not involved in product development. Buyers in this sector may also be involved in monitoring deliveries as well as having direct contact with store managers to receive feedback and guidance on sales figures. Profit margins on the retail selling prices of branded merchandise are usually lower than those of most high street retailers.

Case study in buying branded fashion merchandise

Psyche

Steve Cochrane is the owner and managing director of award-winning independent fashion retailer Psyche, based in Middlesbrough. The two Psyche stores stock branded merchandise in 4000 square feet of selling space, and 20 people are employed within the business. The company was launched in 1982 with the opening of a womenswear store, followed by a separate menswear outlet located nearby. Steve's foray into fashion retailing was originally inspired by his love of music and frustration at the lack of innovative clothing in the region during the early 1980s. At that time Steve had to travel as far as London for clothes that he considered to be either 'different or interesting', so a girl-friend who studied fashion suggested that he should start his own clothing company. Steve was enthusiastic about this idea as he was bored with engineering and was far more interested in clothes and music. He worked in the chemical industry for a few years and then worked 18-hour days for six months on an oil rig to raise the finance to open his first clothing store in nearby Redcar. He does not regret his change of career:

> I'm definitely in the right job now. When I go to fashion fairs, I see people who say 'Oh, not another show', but I love going to them. We've got to go to Florence, Milan and Paris, and we're lucky. You fly there in the morning for a two-day trip and you've got loads of appointments, then fly back the next night without getting to see anywhere. It sounds great, but it's really busy. Yesterday our menswear buyer got the 5.30 AM train to London for a buying trip and got the 7 PM train back, so he had a tough day, but there are peaks and troughs.

Roles and responsibilities

Psyche's menswear buyer has been with the company for seven years and has recently worked his way up to this role. Steve describes him as 'organised and methodical with good IT skills' and considers computer skills and numeracy, including 'mental arithmetic', to be 'crucial' for buyers in this sector of the market. Part of Steve's role is to 'assist' the menswear buyer in the selection of the range. The company also employs a womenswear buyer and assistant buyer. The Psyche team includes a stock controller who is responsible largely for inputting orders, organising deliveries and setting prices, most of which coincides with the buying periods from January until the end of March and from July to September. There is also a marketing manager and a corporate sales manager. The corporate clothing range consists mainly of suits, which are sold to companies for their staff.

As managing director, Steve sees his main job as developing and progressing the company, and safeguarding the jobs of his staff:

> *The business is my baby. I live it and breathe it and work 50 to 60 hours most weeks. I like evolving the shop fit, the interior design of the shops, it's a bit of a labour of love. I spend far too much time and money on it. I don't always like working on the shop floor as I want to work on the business, rather than in it. I'm very keen on learning about garment manufacture and I know quite a bit about it now. I like the buying and marketing, but I like business systems too, looking at the accounts and having management control. For a half-year, it costs £250 000 just to open the doors of our shops, before you sell anything.*

The buying cycle

The buying cycle for menswear at Psyche starts when the buyers visit *Pitti Uomo*, the Florence-based menswear show, in early January or June, followed by the catwalk shows in Paris. Steve particularly enjoys this aspect of his role:

> *Not many British buyers go to the Paris shows, but I go there because I like it. That's the icing on the cake for me. The big stores are always there, like Selfridges and Harvey Nichols, but not many independents go, mainly because of the expense. You used to have to go to Cologne for mens' wear as well, but now Pitti Uomo's the main focus. We go to the shows and make notes, then visit the showrooms and make more notes, plan orders provisionally, then get back, add it up and see how it fits in with our target. We also take photos of some of the styles and show them to the managers to see what they think, especially if we're a bit doubtful.*

Most of the brands stocked by Psyche have show rooms in London, but some are shown only in Milan. The buying period for a spring/summer season starts during the previous June, then goes on until the end of August. For autumn/winter it begins in January and ends around the middle of March. At Psyche the buyers are responsible for checking the selling prices of the merchandise on the shop floor, and that the garment quality is as good as the original samples. All of the staff help to check the quality of the merchandise and if any faults are found many brands will replace stock within about two weeks of delivery or offer a refund. The buyers monitor which styles are selling well and they often need to re-order quickly as there may be only a small quantity of pieces left with the supplier. If a garment is a bestseller for Psyche the situation is likely to be the same in other stores too, and the style will therefore be in demand. Steve believes that, through experience, buyers learn to know on-the-spot which styles will be winners. He finds that useful sources of information for predicting sales include networking with buyers from other stores, particularly at trade shows, viewing the inspiration boards at trade fairs, and reading trade magazines. The price of a garment and the brand's marketing strategy are very important factors for Steve when making buying decisions:

We know our threshold prices. We know it's difficult to get over £100 for a pair of trousers and we know that £60 is a high volume price for us. If we found a pair of trousers that were £20, were reasonably made and we thought we could get £60 for them, we'd be very happy. Branding isn't as important on bottoms as it is on tops. It's a case of looking at the finish, looking at the fabric, when do they deliver and have they got any marketing? We ask them lots of questions. Some brands only deliver 50 per cent of the merchandise we've ordered, and the contracts are weighted in their favour. We ask if it's good value, and how much they'll spend on marketing and where. This is one of the main criteria when we choose to stock a brand. Sometimes they do co-operative marketing with us, by listing us as one of their stockists, or if we took space in a local periodical they could share the costs with us. Some of them will do in-store merchandising or staff-training. Hugo Boss are by far the best at that. They're very successful and they deserve to be.

The buyers plan budgets and arrange meetings attended by the store managers, supervisors and buyers to discuss the new ranges. Steve encourages input from all of the team during these meetings:

We always argue about it. The buyer always wants to buy higher fashion and the store manager always wants to stock commercial styles, because the manager wants to sell everything, but the buyer wants to put his identity on it. It's so easy to buy glamorous clothes that look amazing but don't sell because they're too expensive. The key is getting something that's cheap but looks a lot more than that, so you can get more margin out of it and sell it all at full price. We've stocked very famous Italian labels, which we call 'image labels', that only had 50 per cent sell-through. You get the money back on them, however, because they're great to help you sell the rest of your merchandise. You get the aspirational customer who comes in and can't afford the well-known label, but buys a similar thing from another label. You've got to be able to budget and ruthlessly prioritise what you buy. Every buyer I've ever met goes over budget and swears that the stock is fantastic and will sell well, but a shop can only physically sell so much and they all get carried away.

The buyers at Psyche normally keep aside about 10 per cent of open-to-buy to spend during the season, for 'doing deals' and for buying 'must-haves and winners' that might have been missed. Some brands ring buyers shortly after the beginning of a season to offer stock at 30 to 35 per cent lower than the standard cost price enabling a good margin to be achieved, which can sometimes result in a profit even at sale prices. The buying team always compare sales figures to the previous year. Steve explains that most of the merchandise is expected to sell at full-price in the store:

65 per cent pre-sale sell-through means we only sold 65 per cent at full price prior to the sale, and we're supposed to sell 75 per cent at full-price with 25 per cent going into the sale. The buyer has to predict sell-through, and if it's less than 75 per cent, he has to ask why and there can be good reasons for this. A brand of jeans that we stock is predicted at 85 per cent sell-through, so that means he's going to nearly sell out of it, and only a tiny percentage will go into the sale. If he does that, he gets a big pat on the back and he also gets a buyer's bonus for anything over 75 per cent.

With new brands Steve accepts that it can be difficult to predict sell-through rates, and in his experience it is extremely rare for any brand to have 100 per cent sell-through. The store usually has a '2.5 mark-up', which means the price charged by the supplier is multiplied by 2.5. However, if the mark-up is increased, for instance to three times the supplier's price, the percentage of sell-through needed to make a profit on the style reduces to under 75 per cent. The mark-up in Psyche can vary slightly depending on the brand. A brand with a four times mark-up will make a profit even if only 60 per cent of the merchandise is sold at full-price. The bestselling brands for Psyche in 2000 included Duffer, Armani, Ted Baker, Burberry, Paul Smith, Patrick Cox, Aquascutum and Givenchy. The Psyche sales team are given bonuses for high sales figures and there is a colleague of the week award, with spot prizes of a bottle of wine or store vouchers. Steve feels that there is a distinct difference between ranges of branded fashion merchandise and ranges in the high street fashion multiples:

In the high street, they make things to a price, so if they want a T-shirt at £11.99, designers come up with some ideas, and they amend the style by saying: 'Lose that and that'. Everything on the high street to me is made down *to a price, whereas branded is made* up *to an image, so that's the difference.*

The buyers compile sell-through reports at the end of each season listing the top ten and bottom ten sellers with an explanation of the low sales figures for certain brands. If there is a 79 per cent sell-through, the buyer has under-bought by 4 per cent, and if there is a 68 per cent sell-through, it's been over-bought by 7 per cent. Over-buying can be due to a specific factor such as making the wrong selection of colours in a style. The buyer has to analyse the sizes historically, for example reviewing whether or not women's size 8s sell and whether it is worth stocking them. Steve describes the effect of size ranges and colour selection on sales figures:

We weren't selling 28 inch waist trousers for men, so we start at 30 inch and we're starting to sell 40 inch waist now, because we're getting asked for it, so our sizes are getting bigger, and we've got to analyse that every season. We've also got to analyse what colours sell. We've found we never sell green, no matter whether it's 'in' or not, except for olive for menswear or womenswear. I think the next worst colour is yellow, but we had a fantastic season in summer 2000 with pink for both men and women, and sold out of pink shirts for men, apart from the really bright ones.

Steve attends some of the appointments with his buying team. After the buyers have ordered the goods on buying forms (see Figure 10.2) they have to predict sell-through. They enter the orders into the computer and analyse what they are buying as they go along, so if 500 pairs of shoes have been bought for autumn and sell at a rate of 20 pairs per week, that would be enough to last for 25 weeks. This would mean that too many had been bought, because buyers usually aim for only 10 weeks' cover per style.

After a couple of weeks into the season, the buyers review the sales figures, then re-order the fast sellers. After five weeks, if they have sold half of the opening stock, they are on target. Steve prefers to reduce the price of a poor seller at an early stage of the season by 10 per cent, rather than waiting until the end of the season and halving the price. This would mean the cost price of the garment would be covered, but there would be no contribution towards the overheads of running the company.

Our mark-up is usually only 2.5, compared to three to four times on the high street, but it's branded merchandise and you're paying a premium to have that brand. It's the brand that makes the money, not the retailer. That's why we stopped selling our own Psyche brand. It sold well in other shops, but not in here because it was seen as our own label, so we learned that the hard way. We still produce corporate wear, and we still do small runs of things, our own tailoring and shirts, but we've scaled it down and we don't have a big design team. When you sell your products to other clothes shops, it's a nightmare because you don't get paid. I still have got a sea of post-dated cheques, but with this corporate business you get paid virtually straight away because they're big companies. So many small clothes shops open and close at such a fast rate and they live hand-to-mouth. Some that we have dealt with have gone bust, and we're still owed money in September for deliveries that we sent in February – so by the time I've paid the interest for that, the margin's gone.

Customers

Customer surveys are implemented in Psyche annually, asking for opinions on the layout of the store, customer service, prices and brands. The main aim of the survey is to establish a customer profile. Steve was surprised to find from the 1999 survey that the average age of the Psyche customer was 29, as he had expected customers to be younger.

Chapter 11
Fashion Marketing for Buyers

The purpose of marketing is to maximise a company's sales by selling products which meet consumers' needs effectively. Easey (1995) states that: 'a central component of the definition of fashion marketing is satisfying customers' needs profitably' (p.43). Marketing is not confined solely to promotional strategies, but can be applied to a wide variety of activities within a company, including the product development process in which the buyer plays an important part. This chapter explains those aspects of marketing in which the fashion buyer is regularly involved. When selecting a fashion range, the buyer has to constantly consider the customer's needs in relation to the product, in order to make the range a commercial success. The market for a fashion product comprises all of the potential buyers and sellers of the product, i.e. customers and retailers. It is an integral part of the fashion buyer's role to be familiar with the type of customers at which the product is aimed, and to be aware of similar product ranges offered by competitors.

The fashion marketing mix

The marketing mix is the combination of variables that contribute to the ability of a brand or product to meet consumers' needs profitably, often referred to as the four Ps (see Figure 11.1).

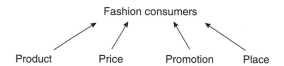

Figure 11.1 The fashion marketing mix.

Every fashion brand has its own unique marketing mix, with each of the four Ps contributing to the customer's perception of the brand's image. Fashion buyers have a significant influence on the product and price elements of the marketing mix of fashion brands and products. The marketing mix for Marks and Spencer's clothing can be briefly summarised as follows:

- Product – menswear, womenswear and childrenswear, including outerwear and underwear ranges, with a reputation for good quality merchandise.
- Price – middle mass market.
- Promotion – word-of-mouth, press and TV advertising, in-store promotions.
- Place – variety chain store with several hundred outlets in the UK, based in town centres and retail parks, and numerous branches overseas.

When a buyer selects the products to be sold by a fashion retailer, it is essential that decisions made in relation to the product reflect the perceived needs of the customer. Buyers have to resist the temptation to allow personal taste to intrude on such decisions, particularly if they are in a different age bracket from the store's potential customers. Buyers play an influential part in determining the selling price (and negotiating the cost price) of the product, and this also needs to be a customer-focused decision. The buyer's input to the promotion of the range is usually limited to the provision of press samples, unless the company operates as a small independent retailer, where the buyer may also be responsible for PR and advertising. 'Place' refers to the method of distribution of merchandise to the customer, which is largely through retail multiples or mail order for fashion products, as detailed in chapters 8 and 9. The buyer's contact with the company's retail outlets is usually restricted to occasional visits to stores.

The fashion product life cycle

Fashion products have a limited life cycle, more so than most other products. The buyer needs to anticipate the expected life cycle of a fashion product in terms of the number of phases or seasons for which it is offered to customers. The product's life cycle may be extended by amending a style gradually from one season to the next, by offering new colourways or adding styling details. The product life cycle (see Figure 11.2) can be applied to a generic product type, or to a specific style stocked by a retailer. Jeans are probably the longest surviving example of a classic item, having been introduced in the nineteenth century, before entering the growth stage as a mainstream fashion item in the 1950s and are currently positioned in the maturity stage. Within the jeans market, boot-cut jeans are also in the maturity stage, having been re-introduced to the mass market in the mid 1990s, based on styling from the 1970s.

Even within such a classic product area there are fads, such as the short-term fashion for the hems of jeans to be decorated with feathers and beads, inspired by Gucci, in 1999. Fads evidently have a shorter product life cycle than classic styles and the buyer needs to predict the length of this timespan precisely to assist range planning. The product life cycle can last from four weeks up to

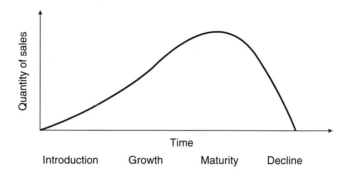

Figure 11.2   The product life cycle.

several decades but for most women's fashion styles it is likely to last from six months to a year. Most menswear and childrenswear styles have a longer product life cycle than womenswear items though girlswear is responding increasingly quickly to mainstream trends. A concept closely linked to that of the product life cycle is opinion leadership, the theory that opinion leaders within society are the first to experiment with new styles before they are seen and later adopted by the mass market.

Introduction

Most new fashion styles are introduced at designer level. At this stage the product is obviously in a high price bracket and only available to a limited number of customers. The style may then be promoted through press coverage of runway shows which generates interest from fashion consumers. Buyers and designers identify products which are at the introduction stage of the product life cycle on directional shopping trips and through fashion forecasting information. Buyers working for stores which sell contemporary designer-level merchandise can rely mainly on instinct and experience to decide which styles to stock, as most of their products are at the introduction stage, and the minority are in the growth stage, of the product life cycle.

Growth

A limited number of the numerous fashion styles introduced in designer ready-to-wear ranges are adopted by the mass market. During the growth stage of the product life cycle, versions of these styles become available in the more fashion-conscious high street multiples. As designer ranges are shown on the catwalks almost six months ahead of a season this often gives the mass market the opportunity to introduce similar styles within the same season. The promotion of mass market fashion products within the fashion press usually peaks within the growth stage.

Maturity

In the maturity stage of the product life cycle a style is stocked by an increasing number of mass market stores and the maximum sales volume is achieved. At this stage the style may be diluted by conservative or lower price-bracket retailers, and variations may be introduced by fashion-led retailers. The maturity stage may be protracted for several years if the style becomes a classic item.

Decline

In the decline stage of the product life cycle a style is likely to be discounted to ensure that sales are made whilst it remains a wearable item for fashion consumers. A classic item may have a long decline stage. Since many fashion items from previous decades are subsequently revived, some styles may re-enter the introduction stage of the product life cycle within a relatively short period after decline.

Customer profiles

Most fashion retailers define the type of customer at whom their products are aimed, describing them as potential or target customers. The potential customers may not currently shop at the buyer's store but include the type of customer to whom the company aims to sell its products. Focusing on a particular area of the market in this way is referred to as market segmentation. It is usually the responsibility of a retailer's marketing department to specify customer profiles and give buyers and designers an overview of the type of consumer for whom the product ranges should cater. Customer profiles are usually brief written descriptions of potential customers but can also be compiled visually in the form of a collage. The key elements which can be contained in customer profiles include:

- demographic segmentation: factual information such as gender and age group;
- psychographic segmentation (lifestyle): type of employment, family aspects, type of housing, typical holiday locations, likes and dislikes;
- geographic segmentation: typical locations for customers, cities, towns, villages and type of housing.

A customer profile can be approached in various ways. Often it describes the typical customer, also known as the core customer, who shops at the specified retailer's stores. This could take the form of a description of an average customer who can sometimes be given a fictitious first name. Customer profiles can also be broader to incorporate several types of the retailer's customers. Some companies prefer to focus on the customer's aspirational life style, rather than the life which most of them actually lead, as fashion very often reflects customers' aspirations. Fashion retailers have many customers in addition to the core customer who may be older or in a lower income bracket than the typical customer whom the buyer is targeting. Life style is increasingly superseding age as the most important factor in product selection, and a retailer which aims at a core age range of 25 to 35 will probably find in practice that they have customers aged from 15 to 70. However it is still necessary to aim the range primarily at 25- to 35-year-olds, as this is likely to be the age bracket in which many of those younger and older customers would like to be.

It is important for retailers to review the life style and tastes of the potential customer regularly if they wish to maintain a particular age range. Maintaining a consistent group of customers can be a risk as the group's customer profile will age and they will become less likely to take an interest in fashion. This type of scenario may have contributed to the financial problems at Laura Ashley in recent years. Targeting an older market segment, such as the over 55s, can also be a profitable venture as many people in this bracket have reached the peak of their earnings, own their own homes and no longer have dependent children, resulting in a high disposable income which could be spent on clothing.

The income bracket of the customer can be less crucial than it first sounds, as it often does not correlate with the amount of money he or she is prepared to spend on clothes. High earners may not consider clothes to be a spending priority, perhaps because most of their time is devoted to work or they may have large financial commitments such as a mortgage. Conversely a low earner, particularly in the younger age group, may prioritise spending on clothes due to lack of long-term financial commitments and more time available for socialising and so have a relatively high disposable income. Buyers need to be familiar with customer profiles to ensure that they aim ranges at the relevant life style, considering where, when and why certain garments will be worn. If the retailer is targeting customers at management level this will probably be reflected by including formal office wear such as classic tailoring in the range, at a middle to high price bracket. A younger target customer in a lower income bracket, on the other hand, is likely to require clothing primarily for socialising, such as leisurewear and clubwear.

Marketing research methods

Some fashion retailers undertake market research to define their potential customers or to find consumer opinion on the product range. This may be done by the retailer's own marketing department or it may be carried out by an independent marketing research company. Research which is exclusive to one company and may involve contacting customers directly is referred to as primary research (or field research). Secondary research involves looking at information and data which have already been published (also called desk research). Despite its name secondary research usually happens first as it can be much quicker and more economical to seek existing information. However primary research is often the only appropriate method to use particularly when the aim is to find out the opinions of specific types of customer on certain products.

Primary research

Methods of primary research include:

- surveys by questionnaire, either face-to-face or by post;
- focus groups;
- interviews.

The focus group is a popular method for eliciting consumer opinions and involves the careful selection of a group of potential or actual customers who are asked a series of questions or given topics for discussion. This can result in in-depth information but must be regarded with caution as due to the small size of the sample it is not necessarily representative of most customers. This can be overcome partly by planning several focus group sessions with different participants, possibly in different cities, to allow for geographic differences. With all market research it is important that the researcher aims to be unbiased (though this is never entirely possible) to gain realistic and useful consumer feedback. Researchers should not offer their own opinions or try to guide the participants to anticipated responses. Even stating the name of the retailer could influence customers favourably towards a range as participants often have a natural willingness to give the 'right' or expected answer. For this reason, it may be best to use an independent marketing research company.

The results of market research surveys are only as good as the questions which have been asked and the professionalism of the market research team. Though market research is generally the responsibility of the marketing department, buyers can initiate informal market research by gathering a group of the retailer's customers in a focus group to request opinions on a range which is currently being developed.

Store visits and comparative shopping

It is an integral part of most buyers' jobs to visit branches of their own retailers' stores and this can be categorised as primary research. Store visits involve speaking to salespeople who can give valuable feedback from constant direct contact with customers. This could enable a buyer to discover why a particular garment or range did not sell well, or conversely, the factors which contributed to the successful performance of a range. The best times to visit store branches are just before the development of a new range so that the buyer can learn from current successes and mistakes, or during a markdown promotion when the store is likely to be full of customers. Oasis sends members of buying teams from management to trainee level to stores for a day, to act anonymously as assistants in the changing rooms, which gives them first-hand experience of customers' responses to their ranges. Ideally a buyer should visit stores several times per season at different branches to become familiar with various types of customer.

'Mystery shoppers' are also used by some stores to gain anonymous feedback from customers which is fed back to the buying department. Some retailers also allow sales or design personnel from their garment suppliers to undertake store visits in their own branches. This offers them direct access to feedback on the ranges which they have designed and manufactured and influences the way in which they develop future ranges for the retailer. Comparative shopping trips were discussed in Chapter 3 and are essential for the buyer to gain knowledge of the products and services on offer to the customer within competing stores.

Secondary research

Sources of secondary research for fashion markets include:

- *Market Intelligence* (Mintel)
- *Retail Intelligence*
- Reports (The Stationery Office)
- *Retail Directory of the UK*
- Annual Company Reports
- Trade magazines, such as *Drapers Record*

Mintel is published monthly and offers overviews of UK markets for specific products of many types including fashion markets such as womenswear retailing, footwear and lingerie. It includes information such as the estimated market value and the main competitors within the market. *Retail Intelligence* (Mintel) has a similar format, focusing exclusively on sectors of the retail market. UK government reports are published by The Stationery Office and can be purchased directly or found in libraries. There are several Stationery Office reports of relevance to fashion markets including 'Regional Trends', which details the average amount of disposable income available to a particular age group and the amount of money spent on average *per capita* on clothes in a particular region. This could influence a fashion retailer to decide on a particular area in which to open a new branch. Fashion trade magazines such as *Fashion Weekly* and *Drapers Record* often include articles about particular market sectors.

The *Retail Directory of the UK* lists multiple and independent retailers of all types including fashion stores, with information such as the location of the head office, the number of outlets and annual turnover; a European edition is also available. This is very useful to retailers who wish to have more knowledge of their competitors, students who wish to apply for jobs and for manufacturers wishing to contact potential new customers. All public limited companies publish annual reports which are available to the general public either by requesting a copy from head office (usually free of charge) or via the company website. The annual report is largely financially based, containing a profit and loss account and balance sheet for the previous year, but it will also summarise subsidiaries of the company and types of product with the intention of enticing potential shareholders to invest in the business. Fashion students will find most if not all of the above publications in university libraries.

Test-marketing fashion products

Certain retailers test-market fashion products by selling them in a limited number of branches in advance of the season. Only large retailers like Marks and Spencer are able to do this because the quantity that would be produced for test marketing (perhaps 500 pieces of a style) can be equivalent to the amount for a total order in a smaller retailer. Test-marketing fashion products can be difficult as customers are influenced by contemporary styles and if they are shown garments ahead of the season they may not be able to anticipate what they will want to wear at that time. Test-marketing can be more useful when launching product concepts which are new to the store (such as an interiors range or nightwear) by trialling them in a representative sample of stores in the first season, minimising the expense and possible risk of introducing the concept to all stores immediately. Independent retailers can test-market products by inviting customers to fashion shows where samples of new styles are modelled and discounts offered for advance orders. Preview mail order catalogues are sent by Next, Grattan and George to a selected group of customers in order to predict demand for a new season's styles, offering discounts to encourage purchases.

Fashion consumer behaviour

The buyer should consider carefully the factors which persuade consumers to purchase fashion products. When buying, customers seek to meet physiological needs such as warmth and comfort, and psychological needs such as improved self-esteem or status. There are the obvious tangible elements to a garment including fabric (handle, weight and texture), fit, trims, embellishment, colour, quality of manufacture, brand name, sizing and price. Non-tangible elements such as image, identification with a peer group, status, aspirations, credibility, exclusivity, style and more practical elements such as comfort and washability can have even more influence on the customer's decision to purchase a garment.

The fashion buyer should take these non-tangible elements into account when developing products rather than focusing narrowly on the more tangible aspects of clothing. The importance of these factors in garment purchase can vary depending on customer type. A younger image-conscious customer is probably more influenced by credibility and peer-group acceptance than an older customer who may prioritise practical considerations instead. The same customer may prioritise factors differently depending on the purpose of the garments; a woman in middle management may spend most of her clothing budget on clothes for work where her status and career aspirations are reflected in her choice of outfits, and she may spend less on leisurewear for the weekend when practicality and comfort are important when she is spending time with her children.

Because customers do not change their whole wardrobes every season changes to a garment range need to be incremental – the extent of change depends on the potential customer at whom the range is aimed and how quickly they respond to fashion trends. At the more innovative end of the market customers are looking for new merchandise at the introductory stage of the product life cycle, but the customer will probably choose to wear new purchases with garments from previous seasons. It is a common perception that, in the womenswear and menswear markets, the younger the customers the more receptive they are to innovation. As discussed earlier, this is not always the case, as life style and disposable income are often more influential than age.

Summary

Fashion buyers have a great deal of influence in the marketing of a retailer's products. In the marketing mix buyers are instrumental in developing the product and finalising prices. Fashion styles have a finite product life cycle which may vary from a few weeks for a fad to many years for a classic item. Retailers define customer profiles to describe the demographics and life style of the consumer at whom the merchandise is aimed. Market research methods may be used to give buyers feedback on customers' opinions of the range. The customer's needs should be considered at all stages of the buying cycle.

Chapter 12
Careers in Fashion Buying

Just as the role of the buyer varies in each organisation, so do the promotional structures of buying departments and the qualifications and career path of each buyer. It is possible for a buyer with a BA(Hons) fashion degree to work alongside another buyer who is a history graduate, and both of them may work for a senior buyer with no post-A-level qualifications. The non-graduate senior buyer is likely to have had retail experience, or to have started work at the company as an administrator picking up skills on the job, both of which may have taken longer than a degree. When employing buyers, some stores will value enthusiasm more highly than a fashion degree.

Having a relevant higher education qualification is not vital for a buyer but it is becoming increasingly important in a competitive retail environment. Most graduates with design-related degrees may initally expect to become designers, but according to fashion recruitment specialist Vanessa Denza the majority are more likely to be employed in other roles within the industry. Students are becoming aware of the central role played by buyers in the development of fashion products to the extent that it is an increasingly popular alternative career option to fashion design. According to a survey of 17 UK higher education institutions by the British Fashion Council most fashion students graduating in 1999 were employed in roles other than designers with fashion buying being second only to fashion design as an employment outlet.

Buyers often travel more and can earn more money than designers and this makes fashion buying a tempting career path for many graduates. Most fashion designers are employed by clothing manufacturers and, with the gradual demise of UK garment production since the 1980s, much production has moved off-shore to Asia. However retailers have remained in their home countries maintaining a consistent demand for buyers, many of whom are expected to initiate product designs when dealing with offshore manufacturers without design facilities. Staff turnover within the fashion industry can be relatively high in comparison to other types of business and many buyers change jobs every two to three years. There are various reasons for this including better employment packages or prospects, being head-hunted, redundancy and internal politics, but boredom is very seldom one of the reasons.

Is fashion buying the right career for me?

Ask yourself whether you are the right type of person to undertake a career in fashion buying. Do not be lured by the potential financial and travel incentives if you are not prepared for the hard work which accompanies these perks. Many of the skills listed in this book can be learned in the workplace but others, such as communication skills, depend on personality. Researching into fashion buying by talking to buyers for example, is useful but you cannot know for certain whether or not you are going to make it until you work in a fashion buying department. Even then, if you find you do not like the job it may be due to the way that your particular department operates at that time or the way in which your line manager works rather than because buying is unsuitable for you. Do not be surprised if you are expected to work long hours even at assistant buyer level as this is the norm in many buying departments. Some buyers have to work weekends when necessary, during an overseas trip or before a key departmental meeting.

If you are unhappy at work you can request a transfer to another department as many retailers offer a flexible career path with sideways moves such as from womenswear to menswear buying. If you have established a good reputation your employer may prefer to keep you in the company by offering an alternative job rather than losing you to another retailer. Most employers will expect their buyers to be adaptable with the flexibility to move to new product areas, and you may be asked to take on a different area without requesting to be moved if your skills are required elsewhere. However if you find that people in other departments are equally dissatisfied it may be time for you to consider applying for a post in another organisation.

Qualifications for a career in fashion buying

There are many different routes into a career as a fashion buyer as shown by the case studies in this book, but probably the most typical route into fashion buying after GCSEs would be to take A-levels (at least one in an art and design subject) and a one-year foundation course. A shorter route taken by many buyers is to take a BTEC National Diploma in fashion (or general art and design) at a further education or art college. After a foundation or National Diploma course the next stage is to enrol on a relevant degree course such as a BA (Hons) fashion design degree or an associated subject such as fashion marketing. A degree will take at least three years to complete. Many degree courses will expect applicants to have gained at least five GCSEs at grade C or above (though some accept a minimum of three), and BTEC National Diploma courses usually require four or more. However, in both further and higher education, 'exceptional entry' students may be admitted with less than the minimum requirements, if they have a particularly strong portfolio of project work or experience in industry or are mature students. Some universities offer a four-year sandwich course which includes up to a year working in the fashion industry. This extra year is extremely valuable as it gives the undergraduate some experience of how the industry operates in practice.

As discussed above and shown in Figure 12.1 there are many buyers who are exceptions to the above routes in terms of education, though, with an increasing number of students graduating from design courses in the UK, it is anticipated that in future a higher proportion of fashion buyers will possess a fashion degree. Several BA(Hons) courses in fashion marketing, product development or fashion promotion have been launched with the aim of producing graduates to work within the fashion business in roles other than design, including buying. Many buyers are graduates in closely related fields such as textiles, or in diverse subjects such as business studies, history or English. If you are currently looking for an appropriate degree course to prepare you for a career in buying check the university's prospectus to see whether buying is addressed within the curriculum, as this is likely to be considered an advantage by employers. Sometimes employees from different departments within fashion retailers, sales managers, head office administrative staff or merchandisers progress into buying. Sales staff can bring with them a wealth of valuable knowledge about the company's customers which may be considered equivalent to a higher education qualification. A graduate who has years of experience in working part-time on the sales floor whilst studying for a degree has a distinct advantage for many employers looking for trainee buyers.

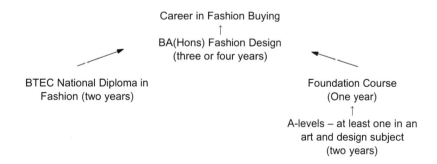

Career in Fashion Buying

BA(Hons) Fashion Design
(three or four years)

BTEC National Diploma in
Fashion (two years)

Foundation Course
(One year)

A-levels – at least one in an
art and design subject
(two years)

Figure 12.1   Possible routes into fashion buying after completion of GCSEs.

Relevant skills for fashion buyers

To achieve a successful career in buying, you will require:

- qualifications or relevant experience;
- effective interpersonal and communication skills;

- decision-making, analytical and numeracy skills;
- enthusiasm for your job;
- knowledge of the relevant fashion market (product, customers and competitors).

As we have seen qualifications and experience are not the only factors which retailers consider when employing buyers but they are the main elements which make one CV stand out from the rest. You may have ideal personal qualities for a career as a buyer but obviously these are unlikely to be noticed unless you manage to get an interview for the job. Gaining fashion retail experience and/or a relevant qualification will therefore give you a stronger chance of being employed in a buying department. If you are suitably qualified retail experience in a different field from fashion may also be useful in helping you to get an interview. Even if you spent three years working in a restaurant whilst studying for your degree, you can stress the transferable skills which you utilised, such as communication, teamwork and organisation. However working in a fashion store is the part-time job which most retailers or job agencies would hope to see on a CV from a student who is about to graduate and is applying for a fashion buying post. Many students need to work to support themselves but even if you can afford to pay your own way through college it is worth working simply to enhance your employability after graduation. If you have a choice of jobs, you should aim to work for a fashion retailer with a high profile such as a store selling designer brands, or an innovative mass market retailer, which is likely to impress a more mainstream retailer. The experience which you gain by meeting consumers directly will be invaluable in assisting you to make effective buying decisions. Most retailers send their buyers on store visits regularly, sometimes in the role of shop assistants working in the changing rooms, to give them a first-hand and therefore realistic perspective on the customer.

Career progression in fashion buying

Buying positions in companies vary in terms of responsibilities and pay – a buying manager working for one retailer may have an equivalent role and salary to a senior buyer for a different store. Smaller companies tend to have more of a flat management structure, with perhaps an assistant buyer progressing directly to buyer. An example of a typical career progression route is shown in Figure 12.2 (see also case studies of Oasis and George in Chapter 8). Some larger companies may also operate in this way to cut out expensive layers of management. Many large retailers employ buyer's assistants or buyer's administrators (at a junior level to the trainee buyer). Some graduates may consider applying for such positions as a route into a buying career, but only in

Figure 12.2 Typical career progression route in fashion buying.

rare cases do they offer promotion into buying as the work tends to be mainly administrative.

Methods of finding jobs in fashion buying

Finding your first job in fashion buying can be a demanding task and it is important to keep trying, expect some rejection letters and see any interview opportunities as valuable experience. Remember that if you are called for an interview it means that someone considers that your experience and qualifications are suitable for a job. If you are not offered the position, it may simply be that your competitors were more suitably qualified. If you do not get a particular job it is worth contacting the employer's human resources department to ask whether you could have improved on any aspects. You must ask this in a positive and non-challenging way if you are to get a response. You must also realise that they are very busy and may not have time to reply to you.

Fashion buying recruitment usually takes place by the following methods:

- press advertising: fashion trade press, national and local newspapers;
- writing speculative letters to employers;
- word of mouth;
- internal vacancies;
- fashion employment agencies.

Press advertising

Fashion trade magazines, including *Drapers Record* and *Fashion Weekly* in the UK, have specialised sections for appointments which usually run to several pages. Employers often advertise vacancies themselves and even if a current vacancy is not suitable it is worth making a note of a retailer's head office address and a name from the human resources department for future reference. You should consider subscribing to a trade magazine if you are looking for a job as you may be competing with other people to get hold of a library or company copy and it is important that you respond quickly to advertisements. National newspapers are usually used only for senior positions or large-scale graduate recruitment as advertising space is relatively expensive. The local press can be a good source of vacancies in the major clothing industry regions such as London, the East Midlands and North-West. If you do not live in these areas but would be willing to relocate it is worth either buying the local newspapers by mail order or visiting to look at advertisements in the local press. Many newspapers now have their own websites which you could access or you could find out which ones to contact through the relevant *Yellow Pages*. Fashion recruitment expert Vanessa Denza recommends contacting the company if you do not hear from them after applying for a job:

> *If you receive no response from a cover letter and CV or application form, phone or write a follow-up letter. Do not call the receptionist every day. Avoid making judgements as to why you have not heard back. Be persistent but not overly so. If they don't call you, don't assume they are not interested.*

Word of mouth and internal advertising

Press advertising is the most obvious recruitment method to use, but word of mouth is an extremely popular alternative and most buyers are likely to be recruited in this way at some point in their careers. A buyer could hear about a post in another company from a friend who works there and apply before the position is advertised, or a buyer could be approached directly by another retailer who has heard of the buyer by reputation. Garment suppliers can sometimes act as go-betweens in this situation as they usually work with more than one retailer and are ideally placed to be able to recommend appropriate buyers. When a vacancy arises the company will often prefer to recruit internally by identifying suitable candidates for promotion. Some retailers issue their own internal vacancy bulletins so existing employees can be offered opportunities first before the company takes the more expensive route of advertising externally.

Fashion recruitment agencies

Several recruitment agencies specialise solely in the fashion industry. Some concentrate on particular segments of the industry, such as buying, design or graduate recruitment. Most of the UK fashion recruitment agencies are based in London including Denza International who recruit for the fashion industry at all levels including graduates for posts in the UK and overseas. There are also fashion recruitment agencies in Manchester, including Menswear Womenswear, and others located in cities such as Nottingham and Leicester. The agencies often advertise in *Drapers Record* listing numerous vacancies, usually with a brief job title, location and salary. The employers in such advertisements maintain their anonymity, mainly so that other agencies do not approach them directly, and fashion companies with a high turnover of staff may not want this to be publicised. The employment agencies charge the employers rather than the applicants for their services as a company is more likely to be able to afford to pay for this than an individual searching for a job. The agencies are usually paid on results so their recruiters are strongly motivated to match applicants to jobs. Deals between recruitment agencies and employers are confidential and usually involve the agency being paid a percentage of the employee's annual salary by the employer if the individual remains in the job for at least an agreed length of time. The employee is not usually party to the details of this agreement.

Agencies mostly prefer to interview people who apply to them, either in person or by telephone, before putting them forward for a job. This is so that they can make their own assessment of the applicant in an informal interview and can discuss their skills and job requirements. Once you are on the books of a fashion recruitment agency you will be contacted when a suitable vacancy arises and the agency will forward your details to the company if you are interested in the position. It is worth registering with several agencies if you are seeking a buying job. Many of the agencies focus on jobs that require three years or more of experience, some at executive level only, but others specialise in junior positions for graduates. Some agencies use head-hunting tactics to find the right person for a job by directly approaching a buyer with the right experience. You may be approached in this way even though you are not intending to change jobs, either because someone has recommended you or because you hold a similar position within a competing retailer. This can reduce the workload of a recruiter by targeting only candidates compatible with the job on offer rather than searching through many often inappropriate CVs. Some agencies ring retailers' head offices to ask the name of the buyer of a particular product area for which they are recruiting, and receptionists are often not permitted to give out buyers' names in case their staff are being approached in this way. The widespread use of the internet holds many possibilities for improving the recruitment process as websites can be updated frequently, widen the pool of potential job candidates, and offer instant worldwide communication. Some websites specialise in finding recruitment for fashion graduates, allowing them the opportunity to exhibit their work to an international audience.

Writing speculative letters to retailers

It is possible to find a job by writing speculative letters to companies for whom you would like to work. This can be rather time-consuming, but it is possible to find work this way and can be worth the time and effort. Employers can find this useful as being approached by suitable candidates can save them time and money by avoiding the need to advertise. Think about which retailers you would like to target and find out where they are located. It is advisable to write to the human resources or personnel department, as they should be aware of all current and imminent vacancies. If your CV and letter show that you have the skills required by the retailer you may even be interviewed before a vacancy arises, particularly if you are an experienced buyer. You can find head office addresses by looking in *Yellow Pages,* visiting the company's website or reading publications such as the *Retail Directory of the UK.* Another effective method of finding this information is to ask shop assistants in the store's branches; they can be very helpful and may even have a list of staff in the company's buying department to whom you could write. You can also write a speculative letter to an agency enclosing your CV even if they are not currently advertising a suitable post.

CVs

Your CV should be clearly legible and well-presented on a maximum of two A4 pages. The first page needs to be interesting enough to hold the employer's attention and make them want to read further. Consider adapting your CV to suit the job or company for which you are applying, so if the post is for menswear put your menswear project from college at the top of the list of course content. This extra bit of effort could potentially be the deciding factor in gaining an interview. You should begin with factual details including your name, address, date of birth and telephone number/e-mail address. Your employment and education details should then be listed in reverse chrono-logical order with the start and finish dates. If you are a graduate ensure that you give a summary of some of the relevant subjects studied on your course as well as the course title and educational institution, as employers are unlikely to be familiar with the course content. Mention the grades of your qualifications only if they are particularly good (As or Bs and first class or upper second class degrees). List any jobs you have had in the fashion industry including place-ments and part-time employment, briefly mentioning your responsibilities and some of the main elements that you learned from each job. Add any additional skills or abilities at the end of your CV. Employers may be interested in your computer skills, particularly on CAD or word-processing programs, as well as languages.

Interview structure

Many interviews for buyers involve panels of interviewers. This will usually include the line manager for the post who may be a buyer or buying manager and at least one other member of staff, such as a buyer from another product area or a member of the human resources (personnel) department. There are likely to be at least two interview stages with the best candidates from the initial interviews being invited back for a second interview, probably with some different members on the panel. Some of the larger retailers ask applicants who have recently graduated to undertake an aptitude test before they are invited for interview. This may be sent to them by post or take place at the head office, testing written skills, numeracy and product knowledge. Many retailers use psychometric tests before interview stage, where there are no right or wrong answers, but the results can help to indicate a profile of the candidates' inter-personal skills. Some retailers invite graduates to participate in recruitment days that include a range of relevant activities. This enables the company to observe how individuals perform in practice and allows candidates to demonstrate their interpersonal skills with the emphasis on working well within a team to solve a set task.

Advice for interviewees

You may have the ideal skills to enable you to be a successful buyer but you will obviously not have the chance to implement them unless you perform well enough in an interview to be offered a job. Interviewers for fashion buying positions are often surprised by interviewees' lack of preparation, particularly with regard to research into the company. You need to convince the interviewer that you are very interested in working for the company by doing your homework beforehand. Another surprise for interviewers is that some candidates applying for a buying position for the first time have no idea what being a buyer involves. Applicants should expect to be asked this question at an interview, and prepare for it accordingly. By reading this book you will have become familiar with the tasks that take place within a buying department and you should be prepared to demonstrate that you have some knowledge of buying during the interview. Motivation is one of the key skills required for buyers and as it is not always possible to show this through qualifications or experience your enthusiasm during the interview, as well as the amount of relevant research which you have done beforehand, will indicate to the employer how well-motivated you are. Your aim in an interview situation should be to project confidence and competence without appearing to be arrogant.

It is not necessary to rely entirely on your natural ability at interviews as there are many ways in which you can plan to increase your chances of getting the job you want. Remember that many managers have not received any training in interviewing people so if you have learnt how to be a good interviewee you could have an advantage over the interviewer. The following list suggests a variety of ways in which you can improve your interview skills by careful planning. You may find it difficult to remember all of these suggestions, but if you apply just a few of them it may help you to clinch the job.

- Present yourself appropriately.
- Find out as much as you can about the company first, though you will not be expected to know everything. Look at stores, websites, articles about the company and annual reports.
- Anticipate which questions you will be asked and plan appropriate answers. Practise your responses with a friend, if possible.
- Keep up-to-date on trends in the industry – read trade magazines.
- Think about which skills and abilities the employer will be looking for.
- Read your application form and CV again before the interview, to remind yourself what you have written.
- Remind yourself of appropriate questions before the interview.
- Think positively. You only get an interview if it looks like you could probably do the job. You have already been short-listed.

Presentation at interviews

Presenting yourself appropriately is essential in the fashion industry. If your clothing is a little too outrageous this may be interpreted by the interviewer as suggesting that you are more interested in becoming a designer and that buying is therefore a second choice or compromise. Conversely if your clothes are viewed as out-of-date or too serious this may imply to the interviewer that you are not seriously interested in fashion. You need to show through your choice of clothes that you are aware of fashion, but with a touch of formality that reflects a business-like and well-organised approach. This does not necessarily mean wearing a suit, but an over-casual outfit should be avoided. What you should wear for an interview obviously varies depending on current trends and it is advisable to choose an outfit which includes the must-have item for the season in the latest colour. This is literally a case of investment dressing, as your appearance could be one amongst several factors which help to get you the job. If you can afford it aim to buy your outfit from a store which is more fashionable and in a slightly higher price bracket than the company which has offered you an interview. (If you can not afford it it may be worthwhile trying to borrow the money for an outfit, knowing that your investment will pay off if you land the right job.) Take care in choosing your accessories, make-up and hairstyle for the interview, giving yourself a total look with the aim of impressing, but not shocking, the interviewer.

Advice during the interview

- First impressions and last impressions are very important.
- Be polite to all members of staff, not just the interviewer.
- Remember that effective communication means listening as well as talking.
- Ask informed questions about the company.
- Do not argue.
- Tell the truth – be honest, but selective in what you say.
- Do not bring up negative points about yourself.
- Use positive body language (non-verbal communication).
- Give examples to demonstrate your qualities and skills.
- Explain career gaps if necessary.
- Say 'I can' (not 'I think' or 'I feel').

First impressions

It has often been quoted that interviewers make up their minds about whether or not to offer a job within the first ten minutes of an interview and this is likely to be true in many cases. Research has shown that people tend to remember most clearly the first and last things that they are told so you should consider the effect that this will have on an interviewer and ensure that your first and last comments make an impact. The first impression is crucial, but don't let this make you too apprehensive; if you make a mistake at the beginning of the interview just make sure to correct it as soon as you realise you have done it. Sometimes employers are just as nervous as applicants, particularly if the interviewer is inexperienced at interviewing. You should ensure that any contact you have with company personnel before the interview shows you in a positive light as you should expect them to inform the interviewer if you are perceived as a problem applicant. The human resources department will not appreciate it should you complain vigorously at not receiving an application form immediately, and the receptionist will not be impressed if you behave rudely on your arrival. Bear in mind that the receptionist is possibly the only person who is familiar with every member of staff in the company, and has the opportunity to speak to them all on an almost daily basis.

Effective communication during an interview

An effective communicator usually aims to seek a balance by talking for an equal amount of time with the other participants in a conversation. As an interviewee you will probably be expected to speak for more than half of the time as the focus is largely on you and your suitability for the job. You also need to listen attentively and carefully to the interviewer/s. How you present yourself is as much about how you communicate as how you dress. Your careful choice of outfit should help to boost your confidence, enabling you to relax a little. Consider your non-verbal communication (NVC), such as body language, during the interview, as this can say as much about you as your verbal skills. If you perch uncomfortably on the edge of the chair or have your arms tightly folded in front of you throughout the interview you will appear nervous and defensive. Try to achieve an open and relaxed approach, without coming across as too laid-back. Practise this by sitting down in front of a mirror, or asking a friend to observe your posture, and alter your position if you do not appear to be at ease. Smile occasionally if relevant though not too much or it may appear that you are not taking the interview seriously. Make sure you maintain eye contact during the interview, and you should aim to look at each member of a panel of interviewers in turn. Focusing on one person can be a mistake, as you may have identified the wrong person as the key member of the panel and that key person may not be the one who asks the most questions.

Ask relevant questions about the company but don't expect confidential information to be revealed to you. It is acceptable to ask whether they sell more of one product type than another, but they are unlikely to give you very specific details such as the current bestseller in the range. It is possible for you to engage in a little debate on a subject within the interview but it is obviously not advisable to be argumentative, however strongly you feel about the topic. You need to be honest in an interview, particularly when asked direct questions, as the fashion business has its own grapevine, and you should expect to be found out if you lie about something, for instance if you were to say that you resigned from a certain job when you were actually made redundant. However you need to be selective in your comments and avoid advertising any negative points about yourself, so don't mention your weaknesses unless asked. Some interviewers will ask you to explain your strengths and weaknesses, so be prepared for this question. When planning your response, make sure that the list of your strengths is the longest. Ensure that amongst your strengths are relevant qualities and skills for the job and give examples as evidence. Consider your weaknesses and try to phrase them in a positive way so that they appear to be redeemable; 'my computer skills are average, but I want to improve, so I've registered for a nightclass'. During the interview, aim to use assertive and confident phrases such as 'I can' or 'I will', rather than vague phrases such as 'I think' or 'I feel'.

Questions to ask at interviews

Remember that the interview is a two-way process. It is important for the company to find out whether you are the right person for the job and you need to know whether the job will be right for you. Interviewers will usually ask if you have any questions, often at the close of the interview and you could prepare for this by asking some of the questions below. Do not ask all of these questions, but select two or three and prioritise them. If you only ask about the salary, holidays and travel, you could give the impression that they are the motivation behind your application. Although this may be partly true, it would be a good idea not to make it so obvious to the interviewers. You should also prepare one or two questions that are directly relevant to the job for which you have applied. Make sure you have listened carefully to their comments in the interview, as some of the questions you have prepared could have been answered earlier. Try not to look shocked at their responses; if the interviewer says that buyers often work until 7 PM, don't ask whether overtime is paid as the answer will invariably be 'no'. You may wish to select two or three relevant questions from the following list to ask during an interview for a buying post:

- Are you conducting second interviews for this job?
- When will I hear from you about the job?
- What opportunities are there for promotion and progression in this post?
- How many days of annual leave would I have?
- What are the regular working hours?
- Does the job include any travel? (If so, where and when?)
- Would I be based at head office?
- What salary are you offering for this post? (Consider asking this at the end of the interview)

After the interview

You usually cannot tell whether or not you have got a job depending on how well you feel the interview went. Sometimes people are offered jobs when they are convinced that the interview went badly and others are surprised to be rejected after a seemingly positive interview. This is mainly because employers have a wide range of approaches to interviewing and many interviewers purposely take a tough approach to see how the applicant copes under pressure. If you should be offered a post, consider carefully before you accept it. If this is your first job it is a decision that could define the rest of your career. If you can manage financially, don't necessarily take the first job you are offered if you do not feel comfortable about it. If necessary, seek advice from your lecturers, family and friends before accepting a post, but the final decision must rest with you.

Summary

Many fashion buyers have fashion-related degrees, although it is not essential to have studied fashion to take up a career in buying. Buyers need to have a strong interest in fashion, combined with interpersonal skills such as teamwork and time management. Fashion buying jobs can be found mostly through advertisements in the trade press, word of mouth and fashion recruitment agencies. Knowledge of the retailer to whom the candidate has applied for a job, an awareness of the buyer's role, and careful planning can be advantageous when being interviewed for a buying position.

Bibliography and Further Reading

Bibliography

Easey, M. (1995) *Fashion Marketing*. Blackwell Science, Oxford.
Mintel Retail Intelligence (1999) *Womenswear Retailing*. Mintel Publications, March edition, London.
Stone, E. (1987) *Fashion Buying*. McGraw Hill.
Tyler, D. (2000) *Carr & Latham's Technology of Clothing Manufacture*, 3rd edition. Blackwell Science, Oxford.
Wells, K. (1997) *Fabric Dyeing and Printing*. Conran Octopus, London.

Further reading

Chuter, A.J. (1995) *Introduction to Clothing Production Management*, 2nd edition, Blackwell Science, Oxford.
Cooklin, G. (1992) *Introduction to Clothing Manufacture*. Blackwell Science, Oxford.
Cooklin, G. (1997) *Garment Technology for Fashion Designers*. Blackwell Science, Oxford.
McKelvey, K. (1996) *Fashion Source Book*, Blackwell Science, Oxford.
McKelvey, K. (1998) *Illustrating Fashion*. Blackwell Science, Oxford.
Rouse, E. (1989) *Understanding Fashion*. Blackwell Science, Oxford.

Periodicals

The *Journal of Fashion Marketing and Management*, published by Henry Stewart Publications, includes some very relevant articles on subjects related to fashion buying. Trade magazines are the prime source of published information for the buyer, largely due to the constantly changing nature of fashion. Buyers should read *Drapers Record* regularly to remain informed of developments in the fashion industry. *Fashion Weekly*, another Emap publication, is aimed at the younger, more brand-conscious end of the fashion market. *International Textiles* and *Textile View* are relatively good value sources of fashion trend information. *Collections* is a Japanese publication featuring each season's runway collections, and though it is the most expensive magazine mentioned here, it gives extensive coverage of ready-to-wear ranges. *Lingerie Buyer* focuses largely on branded merchandise.

Though these titles are unlikely to be stocked by provincial newsagents, they can usually be ordered on request. The specialist fashion bookshop, R.D. Franks, of Market Place, London, W1, stocks all of these publications as well as a broad range of international fashion magazines, prediction packages and books on fashion and textiles.

Index